Additional Praise for *Getting Started in Employee Stock Options*

"Don't exercise those employee stock options prematurely! Hedge them. This book gives many practical strategies for ESOs recipients, financial advisors, and tax professionals to maximize the value and minimize the risk of ESOs awards."

—Dr. Linus Wilson, Assistant Professor of Finance,
University of Louisiana at Lafayette

"John Olagues and his creative thinking have always been light years ahead of the typical options professional. In this book, he and coauthor John Summa explain very clearly ways to use the options as your friend in protecting assets. Whether executive or manager, this is a must-read for all employee stock option holders today."

—Robert Duhon, former options trader/hedge fund manager, and former principal in the institutional equity department at Morgan Stanley and Co.

Getting Started in

EMPLOYEE STOCK OPTIONS

The Getting Started In Series

Getting Started in

EMPLOYEE STOCK OPTIONS

John Olagues
John F. Summa

WILEY

John Wiley & Sons, Inc.

Published by John Wiley & Sons, Inc., Hoboken, New Jersey.

Published simultaneously in Canada.

For general information on our other products and services or for technical support, please contact our Customer Care Department within the United States at (800) 762-2974, outside the United States at (317) 572-3993 or fax (317) 572-4002.

Wiley also publishes its books in a variety of electronic formats. Some content that appears in print may not be available in electronic formats. For more information about Wiley products, visit our Web site at www.wiley.com.

ISBN-13: 978-0-470-47192-0

Printed in the United States of America

10 9 8 7 6 5 4 3 2 1

To Caroline and Christine Olagues . . . . . my Beautiful Daughters, who are always on my mind

and my friend and helper Susan Naughton

For Kelemua

and Wondifraw Summa, two amazing and wonderful kids

Contents

Chapter 10

Chapter 11

Chapter 12

Chapter 13

Chapter 14

Chapter 15

Chapter 16

Chapter 17

Chapter 18

Chapter 19

Chapter 20

Chapter 21

Chapter 22

Chapter 23

Preface

Estimates have been made that there are 10 million employees and executives in the United States, and millions more worldwide, who own employee stock options (ESOs). For a significant number of these employees and executives, ESOs constitute a substantial portion of their financial assets, and thus their net worth. Since holders of ESOs do *not* have the choice of selling these assets in a liquid market, as one might do with exchange traded options to lock in gains or reduce potential for losses, a plan for effectively managing ESOs over the long run must become the most prudent course of action.

Yet few employees and executives holding ESOs truly understand the actual and potential value of these assets. For these individuals, this book presents both a valuable source of accurate ESO information and, most importantly, the necessary tools for managing these wasting assets. The concepts and strategies explained in this book will allow grantees (holders) of ESOs, and their financial advisors, to optimize management of ESOs, and to avoid the common pitfalls. The grantee will thus be in a better position to maximize the value of his or her ESO holdings, while effectively managing ESO risk and tax liabilities.

This book, however, differs in at least one crucial aspect from others written on the subject. In this book, the reader will find strategies fully explained, including detailed case studies, involving the selling of exchange-traded (listed) calls and buying of exchange-traded (listed) puts, which are aimed at *hedging the risk of holding ESOs while maximizing their potential value.* As is demonstrated

> **Employee Stock Options (ESOs)**
>
> ESOs are contracts between the employee (or grantee) and the employer (or grantor) that give the employee the right, but not the obligation, to purchase common stock from the employer for a specific price for a specified period of time. The expiration date is fixed on the grant day but may change if the employee decides to terminate or is terminated earlier than expiration. The expiration date is generally ten years from the grant date.

throughout the book, use of exchange-traded options is the best (and only) method available for efficiently and effectively achieving risk reduction while preserving and potentially enhancing the ultimate value of ESOs.

Typically, wealth managers and investment advisors and their tax accountants will recommend as a risk reduction plan the premature exercise of ESOs and sale of stock acquired by the exercise. A profit would typically be realized with the exercise of the ESOs and the sale of the stock. An advisor would probably encourage the use of the net proceeds to diversify into mutual funds and an assortment of stocks, while perhaps keeping some stock in the company for which the grantee works. This can be a costly move.

Imagine yourself owner of Google ESOs that were granted giving you the right to purchase 1,000 shares of Google at a price (strike price) of $300. Now fast-forward two years and the ESOs are vested. You exercised and sold the stock at $650, taking the net after-tax proceeds and investing in a diversified stock or mutual fund portfolio. Your gain would look something like $350 per each share of stock, or $350,000. But you would pay 40 percent of that in ordinary income taxes, leaving $210,000 in net gains after tax.

Given the declines across the board in the past year (2008), however, you could have been down as much as 50 percent, depending on where you parked your money. Suppose your losses on the diversified investment amount to minus 45 percent. This means that your diversified investment portfolio is now worth just $115,500. The $115,500 would then represent less than 30 percent of the "fair value" of the ESOs on the day you exercised them. You paid $140,000 in compensation income tax and forfeited $36,000 of "time premium" when you early exercised. Not a pretty picture, but a move taken by many ESO holders per advice from traditional wealth managers. Had you simply held onto your ESOs and bought some puts to hedge them, however, you would have come out much better.

With some simple hedging using listed puts and calls inside or outside of an individual retirement account (IRA), you could have avoided much, if not all of the large losses from the market decline hurting your portfolio and the payment of premature taxes. Even having hedged the ESOs, you would still have had potential for large upside gains. The hedges would have offset a large degree of the unrealized losses on the ESOs resulting from declines in the market for Google stock. For example, you could have made tax-free money on the puts, which would offset losses in theoretical value of your ESOs.

> ## The Big Picture
>
> The difference in traditional ESO management approaches and an ESO hedging approach is like the difference between driving a 1950s auto without wearing seat belts and driving a late-model auto with seat belts on and airbags operational.

Yet the ESOs you would still hold would have potential for recovery along with additional hedging for further premium capture through call selling. The difference in traditional management approaches and a hedging approach is like the difference between driving a 1950s auto without wearing seat belts and driving a late-model auto with seat belts on and airbags operational. You should get the picture. Old fashion is more than old—it is misguided and potentially very dangerous, financially speaking.

In our view, informed ESO hedging with exchange-traded options will lead to far superior outcomes than use of any other strategy currently offered by wealth managers and financial advisors. With the publication of this first-of-its-kind book, those superior outcomes are now in reach for most ESO holders.

Acknowledgments

We would like to acknowledge the following professionals for their assistance and helpful comments: Chris Murphy, vice president of Credit Suisse, employee options and restricted stock expert; Michael Gray, CPA, employee stock options professional, writer, and past president of Silicon Valley CPAs; Ben Gordon, president of Twenty-First Securities, arbitrage and hedging expert, writer, and columnist; Tim Leung, PhD, assistant professor in Financial Mathematics, Johns Hopkins University; and Ray Wollney, former options market maker on the CBOE and the PSE for over ten years, for his assistance in analyzing many of ideas and concepts that underlie the views expressed in the book.

Introduction

I f you are reading this book, it may be safe to assume you are a holder of ESOs, or advise others who hold them. As you will soon learn, there are choices available to ESO holders that go far beyond the traditional premature exercise plan offered by most financial advisers.

Consider for a moment an example where your ESOs have appreciated in value and you are faced with the choice to exercise them and then sell the stock, on the one hand, or hold on to the ESOs with all the associated risk in the form of possibly giving back gains resulting from the stock declining, on the other hand. Now imagine further that your financial adviser—and maybe you don't need to imagine this—has suggested the early exercise route, resulting in long stock positions that you will then liquidate, to lock in value, and then diversify through purchase of a basket of mutual funds. These are common choices made by many ESO holders and may be one faced by you—not surprising, given that most conventional wisdom dictates this route. Perhaps you are grappling with this question right now. There are, however, other choices available to you.

The central thesis of this book is based on the idea that ESOs have a substantial value on grant day, which is the day they are issued to the employee or executive, and that premature exercises of these ESOs should be avoided because it sacrifices that value, known as time premium or extrinsic value. Avoiding premature exercise is crucial if you plan to maximize the long-term potential value of ESOs.

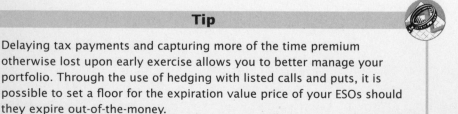

Grant Day

The day ESOs are issued to the employee or executive.

When ESOs are exercised prematurely, a large portion of the value (in the form of time premium) is sacrificed to the company granting them, and another part is paid to Uncle Sam through an early tax burden. Time premium can be substantial, depending on how much time remains on the ESOs and what levels of volatility exist in the underlying stock at the time. This becomes clear in the example presented below, where the grantee, who prematurely exercised his ESOs, realized net proceeds (after taxes) of less than 50 percent of the theoretical value of the ESOs he was holding! The lost value came from two sources—from time premium forfeiture and the early exercise tax liability.

Assume that the exercise price is $20 on an ESO and that the stock price on the grant day was $20 with 4.5 years remaining until expiration. While we need to make some assumptions about volatility and interest rates, they will not alter the basic outcome. If the grantee exercises ESOs at 100 percent above the strike price (i.e., at $40), the net proceeds upon exercise of the ESOs and sale of the acquired stock (1,000 shares in this case) would be $12,000 after taxes. But the theoretical value of the options prior to exercise was $24,526. The lower value resulted from $8,000 in taxes due upon exercise and $4,526 in time premium that was forfeited, giving a total value lost of $12,526. *Thus, over 50 percent of the ESOs' value was lost due to early exercise.* Yet strategies can be deployed for avoiding this, and more importantly producing a superior tax-adjusted outcome.

Clearly, delaying tax payments and capturing more of the time premium otherwise lost upon early exercise is going to make for better management of your portfolio. As you will see in this book, it is possible through use of hedging with listed calls and puts to set a floor for the expiration value price of your ESOs should they expire out-of-the-money, while at the same time you preserve potential for upside gain. This is as good as it gets with options.

Tip

Delaying tax payments and capturing more of the time premium otherwise lost upon early exercise allows you to better manage your portfolio. Through the use of hedging with listed calls and puts, it is possible to set a floor for the expiration value price of your ESOs should they expire out-of-the-money.

With the preceding example as the key objective to keep in mind, this book guides you through the steps needed to avoid the trap of early exercise. By offering the best available strategies to manage (and hedge) ESO grants, this book enables grantees to reduce risks while maximizing ESO value and keeping tax liability to a minimum.

To provide the proper background, we present a full explanation of all the essential ESO concepts, including definitions of technical terms. This is followed by contrasting ESOs with exchange-traded (i.e., listed) options, pointing out their differences and similarities. Since hedging of ESOs is done with listed options, it is necessary to get a solid feel for the basics of these often misunderstood trading vehicles.

With the necessary understanding of both ESOs and exchange traded options, you'll get introduced to the subject of ESO risk and reward scenarios, including the important issue of risk from premature exercise and early withdrawal from an IRA. This is followed by a detailed discussion of tax liability, including issues surrounding the so-called IRS Straddle Rule, the Constructive Sale Rule, the Wash Sale Rule, IRS Section 1221 and the tax implications of early exercise versus proper hedging of ESOs with exchange traded options.

The emphasis throughout this book is not on the design of the company's options plan or the options agreement, except to the extent that the plan impacts the grantees. That said, this is the only book that explains and promotes strategies involving the selling of exchange-traded calls and buying exchange-traded puts to manage ESO positions. Ample use of case studies using exchange-traded call and put options provides an accessible vehicle for understanding the hedging strategies that are aimed at efficiently achieving risk reduction while preserving ESO value. Whether a holder of ESOs or advisor to ESO holders, we trust you will find this book offers a valuable new way of thinking about ESOs and their potential value.

Preliminary Concepts and Definitions

Developing a plan to manage and properly hedge your ESOs requires a grounding in key concepts and terminology related to these assets. In this chapter, therefore, we begin by presenting a brief overview of the important company stock plan (CSP) and options award agreement (OAA), which form the legal framework between the options grantee and employer in terms of rights and obligations. We then provide extended definitions and explanations for related concepts, such as the grant price, expiration date, options vesting, and transferability, as well as a review of the basic components of options valuation.

The Company Stock Plan and the Options Award Agreement

The CSP is a document created by the company and generally approved by the shareholders. The CSP outlines the purposes of the plan, and is an essential part of the contract between the options grantee and the employer. The OAA, meanwhile, also is part of the options contract between the options grantee and the company granting the employee stock options. OAAs generally describe the number of options granted, the options expiration date, the exercise price, and the vesting periods and contain details of the specifics of each individual grant. We will address these concepts in more detail later in this chapter.

> ### Did You Know?
>
> The Company Stock Plan (CSP) is a document created by the company and generally approved by the shareholders. The CSP outlines the purposes of the plan and is an essential part of the contract between the options grantee and the employer.

For example, Google's 2004 CSP, among other things, describes how many common shares are subject to the plan, and sets out the nature of the options grants and the procedure for making the grants. The CSP, furthermore, sets forth who administers the plan and gives information that relates to all present and prospective participants in the CSP.

In Section 1 of Google's CSP, its purpose is stated, which is to "attract and retain the best available personnel for positions of substantial responsibilities by issuing various forms of equity compensation." Section 2 of the CSP then gives a definition of an award as a general term that encompasses stock options, restricted stock, stock appreciation rights, restricted stock units, performance, and other forms of equity compensation.

Google's CSP refers to the related OAA, mentioning that the term (i.e., the time to expiration) of each option will be stated in the OAA and that the exercise price (i.e., the price at which the grantee has the right to buy the stock) and the waiting or vesting period will be determined by the administrator of the CSP, and refers to the form and mechanics of exercising the options and the payment of the exercise price.

Google's Options Award Agreement

The Google OAA gives all the detailed specifics that apply to the options granted by the company to the employees and executives. It covers the specific exercise price and other issues related to exercise rights, the total number of options granted, the vesting terms, the type of options, and the nominal expiration day. Key areas covered include early termination consequences, nontransferability, and tax obligations upon exercise. The OAA and the CSP constitute the sole contract between Google and the employee.

Grant Price

The grant price of the option is the price at which the employee or executive can purchase a specific number of shares of common stock from the company. The grant price is usually the closing market price of the stock on the day of the grant, unlike listed options, which have strike prices at standardized intervals (such as $10, $12.5, $15, $20, $25, etc.), the grant price by definition can be any price (i.e., whatever the closing price is on the day of the grant).

Sometimes if the stock declines substantially after the grant, companies may adjust the grant prices lower for executives. The grant prices of employee stock options (ESOs) have been subject to substantial controversy over the past several years as many executives have been accused of backdating grants to days when the stock was lower. There have also been claims that the stock prices have been artificially manipulated downward to accommodate grants to top executives. The grant price is also called the *exercise* or *strike price;* the latter term typically is used in reference to listed stock options.

Expiration Date

The expiration date of an option is the last day the holder of those options can exercise his or her options. For ESOs, the expiration date is often a maximum of 10 years from the date of the grant. Most ESO contracts provide a premature employment termination clause, specifying that the expiration date of options is accelerated to perhaps 60 days after termination. When making calculations of the value of the options at grant day for a company's cost purposes, the company will use an "expected" expiration day, which is usually considerably earlier than the maximum time as specified in the OAA. There is a movement toward reducing the time to expiration used by companies because ESOs must now be expensed against earnings. A lower time to expiration assumed by the company means the ESOs have a lower theoretical value, and therefore the company shows a smaller expense. So we sometimes see companies using seven years instead of ten years to expiration as the maximum time to expiration. This expected time (used for cost calculations), instead of maximum contractual time to expiration, has significant valuation implications, which are explored later.

In some cases, companies such as Google assume that the expected time until expiration is three-and-a-half years when the maximum contractual time to expiration is ten years. The true value and actual costs to the company are indeed higher when 10 years is considered, and the actual ESO value to the employee/executive/grantees may be much greater than Google's *expressed* costs, in our view.

Vesting of Options

Most employee options contracts have provisions that require the employee or executive (the grantees) to remain at the company in good standing for a substantial length of time before he or she fully owns the options and has the ability to exercise the right to buy the stock. *The time between the grant and when the employee or executive owns and can exercise the options is considered the vesting period.* Usually, the vesting period provision allows the grantee to exercise his or her options in a manner similar to the following: 25 percent of the grant vests and is exercisable after one year; 25 percent after the second year; 25 percent after the third year; and 25 percent after the fourth year. In some cases for certain executives, there have been no vesting periods on certain grants.

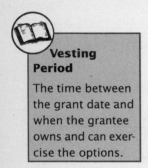

Vesting Period

The time between the grant date and when the grantee owns and can exercise the options.

Transferability

Generally, ESOs cannot be sold or transferred other than upon death or divorce. This provision is part of all stock and options plans in order to prevent the grantee from selling the contract to another party, thereby defeating the intended purpose of the grant. Companies also make the options *not pledgable* so that the grantee cannot use the options for collateral for a loan or to deposit into a margin account to satisfy margin requirements if trading listed options. A few companies actually prohibit employees and executives from trading any puts and calls of the stock of the company. All of these restrictions lower the real and perceived value of the options granted to the grantee. What is the point in lowering the value unless it results in a substantial benefit to the company? This raises questions about the supposed alignment of interest between grantee and employer. If employers have an incentive to lower cost to raise their bottom line, then the grantee is becoming a source of that added profit.

Hedging ESOs

Most wealth managers and financial advisers avoid the subject of hedging ESOs with exchange-traded puts and calls. They refer to several reasons why the client should not hedge his or her ESOs. Even prior books that have been written on the management of ESOs do not tell the grantee how to hedge, although they may introduce the concept. What are the major objections to the hedging argument?

One of the first objections to hedging is that the company does not allow it. However, *most companies do allow it*, even though there are certainly some that prohibit trading puts and calls entirely.

Did You Know?
Most wealth managers and financial advisers avoid the subject of hedging ESOs altogether. But many companies allow it, so do your research. Many of those same managers and advisers recommend premature exercise of ESOs because it benefits them and the issuing company!

To find out whether a grantee is allowed to use puts and calls to hedge ESOs, the grantee has merely to check his or her CSP and OAA. *If there is no prohibition in those documents, then hedging is generally allowed.* Another objection is the claim that hedging ESOs defeats the purpose of the options grant: the alignment of employee interests with the stockholders. Based on the presumption of alignment, hedging is thought to reduce this commonality of interests with the stockholders. That idea may have some truth to it. But hedging may preserve some of the alignment, unless the hedger eliminates entirely the upward profit potential.

Ironically, the common practice of premature exercise of ESOs, together with the sale of the stock, eliminates the alignment of interests 100 percent. But we see no advisers claiming that premature exercise and sale eliminates alignment. Why? Because premature exercises benefit the company and the wealth manager. Wealth managers have the objective of getting assets under management. It would be an awkward moment for a wealth manager to ask for a 1.5 percent fee to tell his client to *not exercise* his options until expiration unless, of course, he can show the potential value added from such a recommendation—something most wealth managers do not understand well. To understand this issue, it is necessary to get a clearer picture of how options are valued.

Theoretical Value

ESOs cannot be traded, but there are some exchange-traded calls that have similar characteristics to a particular ESO. This is not to say that there are exchange-traded calls with exact characteristics as the ESOs. But traded calls can help us determine the value of ESOs, whether the ESOs were just granted or were granted five years ago. In addition, there are theoretical pricing models (Black-Scholes, Cox-Rubenstein, etc.) that have been used for over 30 years to value exchange-traded options, which can be applied to ESOs.

These models, after proper considerations for the differences between the ESOs and standard traded calls, do give, in our view, reasonably accurate values for the ESOs. The accuracy depends on the reliability of the assumptions of expected time to expiration, volatility, and interest rates that are inputs into the theoretical models. It is also reasonable to discount the value of ESOs somewhat for restrictions on the options placed by the company and securities statutes that apply to officers and directors. In 2006, the Financial Accounting Standards Board (FASB) and the Securities and Exchange Commission (SEC) announced that companies are required to value the ESOs when granted and to expense against earnings the fair value at grant day when the options themselves vest.

Fast Fact

In 2006, the Financial Accounting Standards Board and the SEC announced that companies are required to value ESOs when granted and to expense against earnings the theoretical value at grant day when the options themselves vest.

So, to be consistent with generally accepted accounting principles (GAAP), firms must value the ESOs on grant day and expense the theoretical values of the ESOs as they become vested. However, when reporting earnings, companies often report just non-GAAP results, thereby effectively not expensing the options at all—a subject that has generated some controversy and concern about the real value of companies and company stock.

Intrinsic Value

Intrinsic value equals the difference between the exercise price of employee stock options and the present price of the stock, assuming that the stock is trading above the exercise price. The intrinsic value is generally zero at grant day and is always zero if the stock is below the grant/exercise price. An important but often overlooked value dimension, however, is that even *if there is no intrinsic value, there is still value in the options as is recognized by FASB and the SEC and the exchange-traded markets.* We call this value "time premium," which is a very real value, although in the case of ESOs, the value is always theoretical since they do not trade. All listed options that have any time remaining to expiration and that do not have intrinsic value carry a time premium component. Even options with intrinsic value will usually have some time premium. Call options that are far out-of-the-money (strike price is above the stock price) may have tiny amounts of time premium, as do those that have become deep in-the-money (strike price is far below stock price).

An important tax concept is that *the amount that a grantee would be taxed on when exercising his or her ESOs is intrinsic value, not time premium.* The intrinsic value, minus an appropriate tax that is withheld, is the amount that is received by the grantee if he or she immediately sells the stock received upon exercise. The time premium is forfeited upon early exercise and, in practice, represents a lost value, yet no tax offset is allowed.

Fast Fact

The intrinsic value, minus an appropriate tax that is withheld, is the amount that is received by the grantee if he or she immediately sells the stock received upon exercise.

Time Premium

When you take the total price of an option (theoretical or actual) and subtract the intrinsic value, any remaining value is known as time premium.

The time premium of an option will be value added to any intrinsic value due to remaining life of the options, whether the options are ESOs or exchange traded. The time premium may differ, however, depending on the implied or expected volatility of the stock, interest rates, and the expected time remaining until expiration.

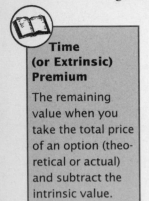

Time (or Extrinsic) Premium

The remaining value when you take the total price of an option (theoretical or actual) and subtract the intrinsic value.

Of course, time premium also depends on the price of the stock in relation to the exercise price of the options. The time premium is greatest on the date of grant, especially when the exercise price is the same as the current market price (considered to be at-the-money). Time premium starts to erode on the first day that the options are granted and continues daily. *Most importantly, the entire remaining time premium is forfeited back to the company when premature exercises are made. It is generally unwise to forfeit time premium.*

Premature Exercise

Simply put, exercises of ESOs that are made sooner than they should be made are known as premature exercises. And, generally, the ESOs should not be exercised much sooner than expiration day, unless an extraordinary event takes place or a relatively large dividend is declared. Making premature exercises of ESOs not only forfeits all of the remaining "time premium" but also incurs a premature income tax that could have been delayed or avoided. *Premature exercising is the primary mistake that grantees make in the management of ESOs.* The premature exercise is similar to an early withdrawal from an IRA or 401(k). But premature exercises are encouraged by many wealth managers.

Premature Exercise

The exercise of ESOs with substantial time remaining until expiration.

Forfeiture of Time Premium

This is one of the very important concepts to understand if a person is going to manage his or her ESOs properly. The time premium is the value above the intrinsic value of the options and is the amount that is forfeited back to the company when a premature exercise is made. Often, the amount is a large percentage of the ESOs' value, especially if the stock is volatile and there is substantial time to expiration.

> **Intrinsic Value**
>
> The value of an option represented by the amount the option is in-the-money. It becomes income to the employee when he exercises.

Premature Tax Liability

When ESOs are exercised with substantial time remaining to expiration, that is referred to as a *premature exercise*. When ESOs are exercised, any intrinsic value of the options is considered compensation income and becomes currently taxable to the grantee. Our view is that there is an economic value in delaying or avoiding the paying of the tax on the intrinsic value and that alternatives to premature exercise should be explored—a major theme of this book.

Nonqualified and Qualified ESOs

Most ESOs are nonqualified, so most of this book focuses on nonqualified ESOs. Qualified options offer the grantee the opportunity to have the profit on the ESOs treated as long-term capital gains. In order to have such a treatment, the grantee is required to hold the stock at least one year after exercising the ESOs. It also requires the grantee to successfully deal with the alternative minimum tax (AMT) to achieve that benefit. Our view is that the proper management of ESOs, whether nonqualified or qualified, requires the avoidance of premature exercises while reducing speculative risk and taxes.

> **Tip**
>
> The proper management of ESOs, whether nonqualified or qualified, requires the avoidance of premature exercises while reducing speculative risk and taxes. With this in mind, then, treat qualified ESOs similarly as you would nonqualified ESOs until expiration day approaches.

The excessive concern for qualified ESO management and the attempt to achieve long-term capital gains is overdone, while the same advisers make cardinal mistakes in other areas. We believe that the best advice is to treat qualified ESOs the same as nonqualified ESOs until expiration day approaches and the possibility of achieving long-term capital gains is examined.

Stock Appreciation Rights (SARs)

SARs are hybrid forms of ESOs. These are awards granted to employees in lieu of cash compensation. The appeal is that the grantee does not need to actually buy the stock from the company and then sell it in the market. The employee is merely paid cash or stock equal to the intrinsic value on the day of exercise.

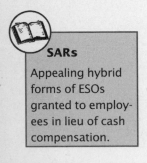

SARs

Appealing hybrid forms of ESOs granted to employees in lieu of cash compensation.

The grantee is merely paid the difference between the exercise price and the current market value of the stock. The payment can be in the form of cash or in new stock issued by the employer. Sometimes SARs are granted separately or in conjunction with stock options or restricted stock. SARs can be valued exactly like ESOs are valued and have vesting periods and expiration dates similar to those of ESOs. For all practical purposes they are equal to ESOs, except that they are more easily exercised and disposed of.

Conclusion

In this chapter, a quick tour through key terminology was provided to establish the proper understanding of the terms required for understanding how to manage your ESOs and how to derive the most value from these assets. By no means exhaustive (the Glossary contains these and additional terms for further reference), it should provide the necessary fluency with the subject of ESOs and their management.

Options Valuation and Basic Concepts

There are more similarities between exchange traded or listed calls and ESOs than there are differences. If a holder of ESOs has any experience trading listed options—maybe as a covered call writer for income or put buying for portfolio protection—the transfer of that experience to hedging ESOs will be a walk in the park. But if a grantee is new to options, he will need some initiation to the basic concepts. This chapter begins with an explanation of exchange traded options and how they work, are valued, and relate to ESOs. For the beginner, this chapter will provide enough knowledge about options so that ESO holders can take the next step toward ESO hedging and financial management decisions. For the experienced trader, of course, this chapter will serve as a review.

How Options Work

In later chapters, we will provide a full explanation and illustration of the main hedging strategies used and referenced throughout this book. Having a good foundation in option valuation, meanwhile, is a good prerequisite. Therefore, in this chapter, in addition to learning the differences and similarities with ESOs and their cousins in the listed options arena,

Intrinsic Value

The part of an option's value represented by the amount that the option is in-the-money. If an option is out-of-the-money, its value is only time premium, and at expiration its value would be zero. If the option is in-the-money prior to expiration, its total value is typically more than the intrinsic value. If intrinsic value is subtracted from the option's full value, finally, the remainder, or residual value, is time premium.

the ESO grantee can get the basics of options valuation. As will be seen, the listed options valuation concepts are applicable, with some minor modifications, to ESO valuation.

It is important that ESO holders get their hands on the wheel of trading, even if just a tiny bit, to make what is a very abstract concept tangible and accessible. At the same time, it is important to read as much as possible but simultaneously reading and doing produces the best and quickest results. Learning by doing is the fastest way to really learn many complicated tasks. Take the example of learning to drive a manual transmission car by simply doing it as opposed to someone explaining how to do it. "Hold the wheel, feather the gas, take your foot off the brake, and quickly but gently release the clutch." After several failed attempts, invariably leading to stalls, the driver eagerly restarts the car and tries again until he finally gets the "feel" for it. This is also true for options. Options require that "feel" dimension to fully "get it." Before that point, however, some options basics are needed. So let's get started.

Did You Know?

Learning about options is easiest with some direct experience. Establish a paper trading account and begin with some simple trading while you study the subject. The learning curve gets shortened significantly when you get some hands-on experience trading paper money or some real money. Keep it small with any real money.

Fast Fact

Time premium, also known as time value, is the amount of an option's value represented by residual value found after subtracting any intrinsic value. Time premium is going to be smaller as the life of the option shortens since its chance of producing a profit in a shorter time frame is lower. The lower chance of a profit means the marketplace will reflect a lower price for that opportunity.

For the reading part of the learning curve, this chapter will help jump-start the process by providing a primer on the essential workings of options. Later chapters will give a look at the relevant options strategies for hedging. The most important thing to understand about exchange-traded options is that they are traded like stocks, futures, and any other instruments. At a very basic level, therefore, the buy-low, sell-high principle applies here like it does with stocks and any other tradable instrument.

Options trade in secondary markets and can be bought and sold in today's online environment for transaction costs as low as 50 cents per option contract. And new margin rules, promulgated by the Securities and Exchange Commission (SEC) in 2006, require lower cash deposits. The rock-bottom commission costs and new margin rules make for an ideal environment for applying ESO hedging strategies using listed options, especially considering how easy it is to execute option strategies online with the cutting edge user-friendly trading platforms now available to retail investors. With a good financial planner helping, finally, it is possible to execute an ESO hedging plan cost effectively.

Volatility

There are two types of volatility (an important dimension of options pricing and valuation): historical (or statistical) volatility and implied (or expected) volatility. The two are important in determining the real value of an option and ESOs, and can be a major factor in calculating the costs of premature exercise of ESOs. The higher the level of volatility, the higher the time premium, and thus costs of a premature exercise.

Understanding Options Valuation

The easiest way to understand the way an option is valued is from the perspective of expiration. While certainly not the whole story, the value of an option at expiration does provide the foundations of valuation from which we can work backwards to assess valuation of options that have not expired. Before we can talk about valuation at expiration, however, understanding some basic definitions is required. So let's turn to some elementary stock options terminology.

The Underlying and Expiration Valuation

The underlying stock refers to the asset from which an option derives its value. In the case of ESOs or listed stock options, the company's common stock is the underlying. The price of the underlying stock is the primary determinant of value, exclusively at expiration. If we know the stock price at expiration, it is simple to determine an option's value if we know what is called the exercise price (also known as the strike price). A call option is in-the-money if the price of the underlying stock is greater than the strike price. Put options are in-the-money if the underlying stock price is below the strike. The value of the option, if in-the-money at expiration, is easy to determine given these elementary concepts.

For example, if a call option or ESO has an exercise price of $40 and the stock price is at $50 upon expiration of the call or ESO, the value is $1,000 ($10 in-the-money × $100 = $1,000). At expiration, all time premium has gone to zero and the only value, if any, will be intrinsic value, the amount that the option is in-the-money. Of course, the potential gains will depend on how much was paid for the options. If $500 was paid for a call option, there would be a profit of $500 ($1,000−$500=$500), or 100 percent return on the $500 investment. With ESOs, however, since they are not purchased the cost basis is zero, so the intrinsic value would be a pure profit or gain.

Pre-Expiration Valuation

Turning to valuation from a pre-expiration perspective, the story gets more complex. To properly value an option at any point prior to expiration, an option pricing model is needed. The most widely used model is the Black-Scholes model. Given the available inputs, it will compute a fair or theoretical value for any option at any point in time. Exhibit 3.1 shows all the inputs that are used to determine an option's theoretical value. Keep in mind, however, that the market price may be higher or lower than the theoretical value, a deviation that may have to do with what is known as *implied volatility.*

EXHIBIT 3.1 Black-Scholes Diagram with Theoretical (Fair Value) Price as Output

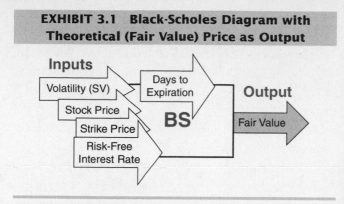

Source: Investopedia.com

Implied volatility is the volatility the options market is expecting and is often different from the actual past volatility of the underlying stock, which is known as *historical or statistical volatility.*

Exhibit 3.2 shows what happens when we reverse the model and plug in the market price of exchange-traded options instead of volatility of the stock price. Here, we solve for the volatility, which is actually known as implied volatility. If the market price used as an input is greater than the theoretical value, the implied volatility will be greater than the statistical volatility. This means the options are overvalued.

With ESOs, however, there is no market price for the options from which to compute implied volatility. Instead, a number must be imported from the listed options market using options having similar expiration periods. But listed options markets don't have options with five-to-ten years' time remaining in them, so some valuation assumptions must be made.

For the most part, however, the mechanics of ESOs are the same as listed options. ESOs (they are always calls by their nature) and listed call options give the holders the right, but do not carry any obligation, to buy the common stock at a fixed exercise price during a limited life span. While certain restrictions often apply to ESOs, these do not fundamentally change the nature of these derivatives from their

Exercise Price (or Strike Price)

The exercise price, or strike price, of an option refers to the price at which the option holder can buy (if holding calls) or sell (if holding puts) the underlying stock if and when the option is exercised. The exercised option forces the seller of a call option to deliver a long stock position, or if a put seller, to receive a long stock position. The call or put holder of an option has the right, but is not obligated, to exercise the option. Exchange traded options automatically exercise if they are in-the-money at expiration by one cent or more. But ESOs are not automatically exercised if they are in-the-money at expiration.

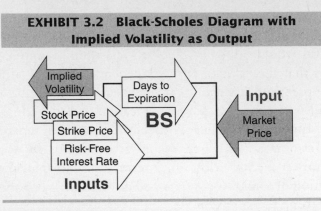

EXHIBIT 3.2   Black-Scholes Diagram with Implied Volatility as Output

Source: Investopedia.com

cousins in the standardized exchange-traded options markets, as we show in this chapter. The valuation equation is fundamentally the same, even if there are some alterations to the fabric of the theoretical model inputs, such as discounting time to expiration. The bottom line is that standard valuation models can be used to derive reasonable theoretical values for ESOs.

Expected Time to Expiration

While ESO and listed options both have specific expiration dates specified in the contract terms, in the case of ESOs, any early termination of employment will shorten the time to expiration to less than a year typically. Let's take two examples to show this point, and its importance.

Suppose that an employee is granted ESOs with a certain expiration date. The employee has the right, but not the obligation, to exercise these call options at any time prior to that date, just as an exchange traded call option holder would have on the same stock. Both the ESOs and the calls are American style. Therefore, it is possible to exercise prior to the expiration date and acquire the underlying stock at the exercise or strike price. Each listed call option represents 100 shares of stock, but with an ESO the amount of stock represented by the options grant is whatever is spelled out in the options agreement. The exercise price for listed options is the same price as the grant price for ESOs, so the stock would be acquired at the grant price of the option.

But if the employee ceases to be employed by the same company, the expiration date would now become closer, and as a result, the value of the ESOs would be reduced due to less time premium. Therefore, this means that the value of an ESO depends on some additional factors. Time premium remaining on an exchange-traded option is always known and is solely a function of the calendar. Yet, with an ESO, the amount of time premium is dependent on more than remaining calendar days. Termination of employment (either voluntarily or involuntarily) can shorten the life of the ESO term and with that, the time premium portion of total value is chopped down. Other factors can reduce "expected" time to expiration.

Other Differences between ESOs and Listed Options

Both ESOs and calls have a value that depends on the stock's expected volatility, the time remaining to expiration, the current and the expected interest rate, and the relation of the underlying stock market price to the exercise price.

Both are considered securities for SEC rules and securities statutes purposes, although SEC Rule 16b-3 generally exempts grants of equity (i.e., ESOs) from Section 16(b) of the Securities Exchange Act of 1934. *The ESO grant transaction is thus considered a purchase by the grantee and is similar to an employee's purchase of listed calls.*

In the case of ESOs, the grantee enters into a contract with the company to issue new shares to the grantee upon exercise. In the case of exchange-traded calls, however, the owner enters a contract with the Options Clearing Corporation (OCC), whereby the OCC is obligated to sell the shares to the owner under the terms of the call contract. One of the most obvious differences, therefore, is that ESOs are *not traded* in a secondary market as are listed options.

Fast Fact

Exchange-traded calls will automatically be exercised if in-the-money at expiration by more than .01 cents. ESOs must be exercised by specific instructions from holders even if in-the-money at expiration.

In the case of ESOs, furthermore, the grantee *cannot* exercise his or her ESOs until the stock options are "vested," a restriction placed on employees for a specified length of time after becoming employed (defined in Chapter 2). With regard to exchange-traded calls, however, there is never a vesting period—a key difference.

The time to expiration of ESOs is generally ten years, whereas the time to expiration of traded calls is a maximum of three years, and most existing calls have one year or less to expiration. Longer-term call options are known as long-term equity anticipation securities (LEAPS), and have expiration dates in January only.

ESOs generally cannot be transferred and generally cannot be pledged to secure a liability or post as margin in an options trading account. Exchange-traded calls, however, can be pledged as good collateral (margin) into a brokerage account and traded (bought and sold) at a moment's notice during trading hours through electronic markets such as the International Securities Exchange (ISE) and Chicago Board Options Exchange (CBOE), among others.

Exchange-traded options can be bought or sold to open and establish speculative positions with either directional or nondirectional profit potential. Similarly, they can be used to construct hedges on stock positions and, as this book demonstrates, to hedge ESOs.

The Greeks

Options strategies have an important dimension known as the Greeks—risk/reward measures that are vital to understanding potential for profit and loss and the effectiveness of a hedging strategy. We finish this chapter, therefore, with a look at the role of the Greeks, beginning with delta, the directional risk and reward indicator.

Delta

Delta measures the exposure to price changes of the underlying stock. It refers to the expected change of an option price as the stock changes a small amount. For example, assume a call has a .50 delta (individual strike deltas range from 0 to 1.0). This means that if a stock that is trading for $100 goes up one dollar in a day (i.e., $100 to $101), the call will advance one half of one point of premium, or $50 (.5 × multiplier of 100 = $50). If we find a put that has a .50 delta given a stock trading at

100, and the stock drops one dollar in a day, the put would go up one half of one point, or $50. Delta, however, is not fixed, and it changes with time premium decay and movement of the underlying stock. But an at-the-money option will have a delta always at or near .50.

In addition to the size of delta, there is also the sign (positive or negative) of the delta. Call options have positive deltas and puts have negative deltas. This means that if a stock goes up so does the call price (holding other things equal) and the put price declines. Just the reverse is true when the stock goes down. Furthermore, if you bought 1 call and 1 put, each having a .50 delta value (call delta positive, put delta negative), the summed deltas would be zero (delta neutral). Delta neutral means change in one option's price will offset the change in the other option's price. When you combine options in a strategy position, you always have a position delta. It may be neutral, negative, or positive.

If holding ESOs giving the right to buy 1000 shares of stock, and the delta of the ESOs is .65, this would mean that the ESOs would have a total of 650 positive deltas (.65 × 1000). If 10 listed calls are sold against the ESO position, each with a .50 delta, the summed position deltas would be positive 150 (i.e., +650 ESO deltas − 500 listed call negative deltas = +150 position deltas). This means that the overall position still has a long bias (that is, a positive position delta) and would benefit from a rise in the stock price. However, it is less exposed on the downside, having just 150 positive deltas instead of 650. This is an example of a partial hedging approach discussed later in this book.

Did You Know?

Two Position Delta Calculation Examples

1. If you held 650 positive deltas from grants of ESOs and bought 10 puts, each having −40 deltas (−400 total), then the summed position would be 250 positive deltas (650 − 400 = +250 deltas). The −400 deltas of the puts is arrived at by multiplying the delta of the exercise price (−.40) by the the number of puts (10) and multiplying that number (4) by a multiplier of 100 (the number of shares represented by each put option).

2. Assume that a person owns 300 shares of stock (i.e., 300 positive deltas) and then did a "qualified covered call" write, meaning the person sold three slightly out-of-the-money calls with a delta of .50 each (for −150 total deltas). The "covered" writer would have total positive deltas of +150 (300 − 150 = +150 deltas). Again, we arrive at the total deltas of the 3 calls using the following formula: −.50 delta × 3 calls sold × 100 multiplier = −150 deltas

All other things remaining the same, the more an option gets in-the-money, the larger the delta becomes. The more the option gets out-of-the-money, the smaller the delta. Generally, the shorter the time remaining until expiration, the more the delta approaches 100 for in-the-money options and the more the delta approaches zero for out-of-the-money options.

If the stock goes down, by the way, the gain in the long puts will be tax-free if held inside of an IRA account but could be long-term capital gains outside an IRA account if held for more than a year. The favorable tax treatment of the gains on puts held inside an IRA essentially makes it such that they have more after-tax deltas than they do if the tax treatment is not considered. Delta is a concept that all holders of ESOs and listed options should understand.

Rate of Change of Delta Risk

Gamma

Gamma is another one of the options Greeks, and it measures the rate of change of delta of the options over a short period of time. Let's say a call option has a strike price of $50 and delta of .50, which gives the holder the right to buy the stock at $50. If the stock is trading at $48, the call will pick up more positive deltas when and if the stock goes up (closer to the strike price or higher). If the stock goes to $50 the delta would then be perhaps about .55. The rate of increase of delta is known as gamma, and it is typically highest near the strike price when near to expiration. So delta is not a constant.

Gamma is simply a measure of the rate of change of the rate of change of an option's price. Delta measures the rate of change of an option's price and gamma measures the rate of change of delta.

Measuring Time Premium Decay Risk and Reward

Theta

Theta is a another so-called options Greek. It measures the change in the value of an option resulting from the daily erosion of "time premium" of an option. The time premium is calculated by reference to a theoretical pricing model, such as the Black-Scholes pricing model, or by simply

	EXHIBIT 3.3 Summary Chart			
Positions	Delta	Gamma	Theta	Vega
Own ESOs	+	+	−	+
Long calls	+	+	−	+
Short calls	−	−	+	−

looking at the market value of listed options. Negative position theta of summed options positions means that the holder of ESOs or option trader will lose money if the stock does not move around substantially and is typically associated with buying strategies. Buying puts, for example, while holding ESOs, creates more total negative theta than already exists. Selling calls, however, reduces the total negative theta (and thus time premium decay risk) that is inherent in holding any ESOs.

Vega

Vega is the last important options Greek and it measures the theoretical price change of an option as a result of a change of one point in the implied or historical volatility of the stock. This means that if you are holding ESOs and the volatility of the stock drops or the implied volatility of the listed calls drops, this will result in a lower value of the ESOs. All long options, including ESOs, face risk from falling volatility. Selling calls (especially long-term calls), however, will reduce the vega risk, and enough selling of options can balance out the vega risk (see Exhibit 3.3).

Chapter

4

Risks of Holding ESOs (Unhedged)

Before exploring issues related to management of ESOs, it is important to understand what is truly at stake with an ESO grant. Too often, employees do not have a grasp of the fundamentals of ESOs, which leaves them unprepared for the potential risks of holding these wasting assets (unhedged). There is a common misconception that the company stock price will rise, when in fact, the statistical probability of ESOs being in-the-money by expiration is actually closer to a coin flip.

Fast Fact

The statistical probability of ESOs being in-the-money at their expiration is actually close to a coin flip.

In this chapter, we present a look at some examples of loss probabilities from holding ESOs and the fair value of these options. Here, we assume no premature exercise or hedging of ESOs, topics to be taken up in subsequent chapters.

A Highly Risky Situation

Exhibit 4.1 illustrates the risk of holding employee stock options that are *not* hedged. Assuming a stock is trading at the ESOs' exercise price upon the grant day, the probability of the stock trading at or below the exercise price upon expiration is nearly 40–50 percent on reasonably volatile stocks (defined as volatilities .30 or greater).

For example, with five years to expiration and a volatility of .30, there is a 40 percent probability of ESOs' being worthless at expiration. If we assume higher levels of volatility, such as .50, the probability rises to 60 percent. This number drops if we decrease the term to expiration, but even at one year to expiration, there is still a 54 percent chance of the ESOs expiring worthless. This makes the holding of unhedged ESOs highly risky, because there is a high probability that the grantee will get absolutely nothing by expiration, as the ESOs could be out-of-the-money and worthless on expiration day. Thus, their equity compensation declines to zero.

These illustrated risks should influence the grantee and his or her advisers to find ways to reduce those risks, especially when the ESOs constitute a large percentage of the grantee's assets.

EXHIBIT 4.1	Probabilities Matrix of Holding Employee Stock Options to Expiration	
Time to Expiration	*Expected Volatilities of the Underlying Stock*	*Probabilities of ESOs Being Worthless at Expiration*
7 YRS	30	40
5 yrs	30	41
3 yrs	30	44
1 yr	30	47
7 YRS	50	62
5 yrs	50	60
3 yrs	50	56
1 yrs	50	54
7 YRS	70	72
5 yrs	70	70
3 yrs	70	65
1 yr	70	59

The matrix in Exhibit 4.1 gives an idea of the risks associated with holding unhedged ESOs if we assume the accuracy of theoretical options pricing models. These models make the assumption that stock prices are log-normally distributed. All calculations are made when the stock is trading at the same price as the exercise price. The expected rate of return is 8 percent.

As can be seen, the more volatile stocks have a greater probability of being out-of-the-money at expiration, therefore making the ESOs worthless.

Exhibit 4.2 presents theoretical values of employee stock options when granted, which is pure time premium if we assume the grant price is the market price of the underlying stock on the grant day. The employee/executive, therefore, subjects himself to the probability shown in Exhibit 4.1 of losing all of the amounts shown in Exhibit 4.2. This assumes the grantee does not hedge his or her ESOs.

We use the Black-Scholes theoretical pricing model with appropriate assumptions. For the data presented in Exhibit 4.2, we assume that the maximum life of the ESOs is 10 years, but we base the calculations on expected life of just 6.1 years. This is done to discount the options value in consideration of expected early employment termination, premature exercises, and lack of transferability. Of course, if the full 10 years were used in the calculation (assuming the employee were to own the ESOs for that length of time), a much larger time premium at risk would be derived. We assume, furthermore, that the market value of the stock is $40, the same as the exercise price, and that 1,000 ESOs were granted, representing the right to buy 1,000 shares.

Exhibit 4.2 gives an idea of the risks associated with holding unhedged ESOs if we assume the accuracy of the Black-Scholes options

EXHIBIT 4.2	Dollar Risk of Holding Employee Stock Options to Expiration		
Number of ESOs Granted	Interest Rate Assumed	Expected Volatility	Fair Value at Grant of 1000 ESOs
1000	3	25	$12,600
1000	3	40	$17,400
1000	3	50	$20,470
1000	3	60	$23,300
1000	3	70	$25,890
1000	3	90	$30,290

pricing model. It assumes 6.1 years of expected life of the options and a maximum life of 10 years. All calculations are made when the stock is trading at the same price as the exercise price with an expected rate of return of 8 percent. The fair value of 1,000 ESOs granted with an exercise price of $40, a maximum of 10 years of contractual life with expected volatility of .70, and an assumed interest rate of 3 percent, is approximately $25,890 on the day granted. There is, at that point, a 70 percent probability that the grantee will lose the $25,890 if he holds the ESOs unhedged until expiration day, as seen in Exhibit 4.1.

Conclusion

Given the large time premium attached to granted ESOs, it makes sense to think about the value at risk. If a grantee does not hedge his or her ESOs, and if the options are out-of-the-money at expiration, there is a loss of 100 percent of value of the options. As we see in the data presented in this chapter, the amount at risk depends primarily on the volatility levels and expected time to expiration of the ESOs.

Fast Fact

If a grantee does not hedge his or her ESOs—and if the options remain out-of-the-money at expiration—there is a loss of 100 percent of value.

Tax Consequences of ESOs

The issue of taxes is one of the most important issues in managing employee stock options and perhaps one of the more complicated and often misunderstood. This is true whether the grantee is an executive or any other employee, whether the options are nonqualified or qualified, or whether the grantee decides to hedge his "naked options" positions or not. This chapter outlines some important areas regarding tax implications related to ESOs, which will give a better feel for navigating the somewhat murky tax waters of ESOs, especially when sitting down with an accountant to map out a plan of action.

If ESOs Are Hedged, Taxes Are Less of a Concern

After a full review of all the tax implications of hedging ESO positions with listed calls and puts, there is only one conclusion that can be drawn: The tax consequences can be highly friendly to the hedger.

When ESOS are "granted" by the employer, there is generally no tax to the employee/grantee (see IRS Section 83) and there are generally no tax consequences when the ESOs vest. Regarding the latter, recall that there are restrictions on the holder of the ESOs, so this generally prevents

Alternative Minimum Tax

A term that refers to a tax assess-able against a holder of qualified ESOs upon exer-cise. AMT is widely discussed in books on man-aging ESOs. Hedg-ing ESOs to reduce risk with listed calls and puts minimizes the concern for the AMT, because we advise not making exercises of ESOs until near expira-tion. The resulting gain from a focus on the AMT is minimal com-pared to the gain from merely de-laying the exer-cise to expiration.

a tax event from occurring. Technically speaking, when ESOs are granted they have no fair market value. Because there is no fair market for these assets, there is no income earned and no capital gains. Keep in mind that ESOs will have zero value upon expira-tion if they expire out-of-the-money.

However, it should be pointed out that vesting of restricted stock is a taxable event because vesting of restricted stock generally eliminates any restrictions on the sale of such stock.

When the grantee exercises the granted options, this becomes a taxable event. Exercising the ESOs, whether the options are qualified or not, produces an automatic tax liability. If the ESOs are nonqualified, the intrinsic value at the time of the exercise becomes *compensation income.* The rate in some states can be as high as 50%. In the case of qualified ESOs, mean-while, the gain upon exercise becomes subject to the alternative minimum tax (AMT).

These early tax consequences, therefore, are compelling reasons for delaying the exercise of the ESOs, perhaps until expiration, especially if the abil-ity to hedge or partially hedge is an available choice to the employee/grantee.

Furthermore, if the grantee holds the stock after the exercise of nonqualified ESOs, any gain or loss in the market value from the time of exercise becomes subject to capital gains treatment. The gain will be long-term capital gain if held more than one year. Any loss will be capital loss. In the case of qualified ESOs, the gain after exercise is treated the same as the gain on stock received from the exercise of nonqualified ESOs. If the stock that is received upon exercise of qualified ESOs is held for longer than one year, the entire gain, including the intrinsic value on the day of exer-cise, becomes long-term capital gain, with appropriate recapture of the AMT that was paid.

If ESOs Are Hedged, Risk Is Minimized

When the grantee sells listed call options to hedge his or her granted ESOs, there is generally no taxable event, although an argument could be made that in a rare event the Constructive Sale Rule may apply (discussed in the following chapter, and in Appendix A). The chance of the Constructive Sale Rule IRS Section 1259 applying is highly unlikely, however, especially if done with the advice of qualified options advisers. More discussion about IRS Section 1259, which deals with Constructive Sales, appears in Appendix A.

In cases where the grantee owns company common stock or other securities and deposits those securities as collateral, he or she can often withdraw all or most of the proceeds of the sale of the calls without a taxable event and without incurring an interest charge from borrowing.

Another form of hedging involves buying puts to also reduce the downside risk to the grantee who is holding ESOs. There is no taxable event upon the purchase of puts. If the puts are long-term puts and are held for over one year, any gain on the put options may be subject to a long-term capital gains tax treatment. However, in some cases when puts are purchased to hedge nonqualified ESOs, the resulting transaction may be subject to IRS Section 1221, where the gains or losses are ordinary gains and losses.

The buying of puts, or the sale of calls to offset existing positions in stock, may create what is referred to as a *straddle* under IRS Section 1092 (the so-called Straddle Rule). If the offsetting positions are considered straddles, that actually creates possibly a more favorable tax consequence. We will discuss this in detail in Appendix A.

Finally, if the grantee uses an individual retirement account (IRA) structure to help manage ESOs and the grantee purchases puts, or does any other hedging combination with exchange-traded options inside an IRA, there is no taxable event on the day the trades are initiated. Any gain inside the IRA is either tax free in the case of a Roth IRA, or tax deferred in the case of a traditional IRA. An argument can be made, however, that any liquidated loss in an IRA from these positions that offset "naked" stock will increase the cost basis of the stock under the Straddle Rule (Section 1092).

Other Considerations

If the grantee sells calls to hedge his ESO position outside of an IRA account and can withdraw the proceeds, he may be able, if eligible, to make an additional deposit of the proceeds into his IRA account and get either a tax deduction or special treatment on the gains that may result from the investment of those proceeds.

Example of Risk and Tax Liability Reduction

Assumptions

Suppose you own ESOs giving you the right to purchase 2,000 shares of ABC Company at $20. Also, assume you own 1,000 shares of previously restricted stock. The stock trades at $40, and both the ESOs and restricted stock are vested. Furthermore, the taxes have been paid on the formerly restricted stock.

If you notice that the implied volatilities on the listed calls have increased substantially (meaning the prices are high) you may want to write (sell) calls to take advantage of the extra premium in the listed calls and reduce the risk of holding the ESO and restricted stock "naked." You are offsetting some long delta risk, in other words. The value of the stock holdings is $40,000. The value of the ESOs is about $52,000 with a positive delta of .87.

Delta

Before any hedging, what is the risk? The equivalent stock position is +2,740 (i.e., 1,000 shares of restricted stock +.87 × 2,000 ESOs). To hedge the long position, you decide to sell 20 long-term calls having two years to expiration with a delta of .67 each and an exercise price of $40. The market value of the calls is $10, or $1,000 per hundred shares ($10 × 100 = $1,000). The total proceeds from the sale of the listed LEAPS calls would be $20,000, and the equivalent stock position after the sale of the calls now would be +1,400 (i.e., +2,740 – [.67 × 20 × 100] = +1,400). Meanwhile, the $20,000 can be removed from your account with no borrowing or interest charges. So you take the $20,000 and deposit as much as you can into a traditional IRA or Roth IRA, achieving the maximum deduction. Make more deposits the next two years into your IRA, using up the $20,000.

Taxes

Have you paid any tax? No, the proceeds of the sale are not taxed until you liquidate the positions at a gain or the options expire out-of-the-money. If deposits are made into an IRA with all or part of the $20,000, you have achieved an ordinary tax deduction to the extent that you make those deposits into an IRA.

Results at Expiration of Listed Calls

Assume that the stock trades at $45 when the two-year calls expire. You would be assigned the exercise notice, and would become short 2,000 shares versus the 1,000 formerly restricted stock.

Effectively, you will have made a profit of $10,000 on the 20 calls that were "written." Your stock position is up five points, adding another $5,000 in unliquidated gains, and the ESOs are probably up about three points, adding some $6,000 in theoretical value ($3 × 2,000 shares). However, there would be no current tax on those ESO profits (unless the 1,000 formerly restricted stock shares are used to cover the short position created by the assignment of the calls). The tax liability occurs only when the short sale is closed at a profit or the long stock is sold.

The outcome of the above positions is that you will have received tax deductions and reduced taxes because some of the deposits to the IRA could be tax deductible. The interest and profits you earn inside of an IRA are either tax deferred or not taxed at all (i.e., in a Roth IRA).

Any Time Premium Forfeited?

Have you forfeited any "time premium" by a premature exercise in the example above? No! You captured $20,000 worth of "time premium," although because of the rise in the stock, the net premium "captured" was reduced to $10,000. Still you come out ahead.

Risk Reduction

Have you reduced the speculative risk of holding ESOs? Yes, you have. Your delta and theta risks are reduced. This is efficient management of ESOs. The tax deduction, or the special tax treatment on the deposit of the proceeds into an IRA, will offset any tax liability that may occur from any premature exercise of the ESOs.

Sometimes when ESOs are nearing expiration and there is little "time premium" remaining, an early exercise and sale of stock may be warranted on part of the position if the intrinsic value earned on the options can be deposited into a traditional IRA, since the result will be a tax deduction, offsetting the realized compensation gain. While the above example may seem complicated, the basic approaches outlined in the book will make clear each step of the process of hedging.

Chapter

Straddle Rule and Tax Implications of Hedging ESOs

When thinking about ESOs and how best to manage them, special attention needs to be paid to the potential tax benefits and liabilities of the choices available to you. While not all the tax implications are obvious (always best to consult a qualified tax accountant), some broad conclusions can be drawn when it comes to management of ESOs.

In this chapter, the case against premature exercise is strengthened by a look at several scenarios involving hedging ESOs and the associated tax implications. As will be seen, hidden in the premature exercise is a substantial tax liability that can easily be delayed or avoided with some proper steps aimed at managing the risk of holding ESOs through simple hedging or partial hedging techniques.

The Straddle Rule IRS Section 1092

Let's begin with a look at a simple example of an offsetting position to illustrate the issue of the straddle rule and how that might affect different choices (i.e., available to a grantee exercise versus hedge). Assume an investor establishes two positions—one in stocks and the other with listed options—so that the positions are offsetting. This investor would, therefore, expect that if the price of the shares moved up or down, there would be a gain on one position offset by a loss on the other position and vice versa. If the investor were in such a position near the close of the tax year, he or she could liquidate the losing side and take a deduction. This was possible prior to the establishment of the Straddle Rule Section 1092 of the U.S. tax code.

Clearly, if the investor liquidated the losing position right before calendar year-end, he or she would have a tax deduction immediately and could delay the gain on the offsetting position until sometime in the future. The IRS created Rule 1092 to stop that practice. The rule says that the liquidated loss in advance of the liquidation of the gain has to be delayed to the future to the extent that the loss is offset by the unrecognized gain on the offsetting position.

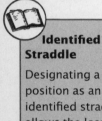

Identified Straddle

Designating a position as an identified straddle allows the loss on the offsetting position to raise the cost basis of the profitable unliquidated position.

The IRS, however, created two ways of handling the early loss liquidation. One way is to have the investor designate the offsetting positions as an "identified straddle." This identification makes it such that any liquidated losses that precede the liquidation of the offsetting position having gains are merely used to increase the cost basis (i.e., purchase price of long stock) of the unrealized gain position. Essentially, this means that if there is an "identified straddle" where one position has an $11,000 loss and the other position has a $15,000 gain, the liquidation of the $11,000 loss is not deductible when it occurs and merely raises the cost basis of the unliquidated position by $11,000.

Example
MasterCard

Assume that MasterCard stock is trading at $144 as it was in March 2009. Assume also that an investor is long 500 shares. She decides to sell five calls with an expiration date two years from March 2009 and a strike price of $120. She receives $4,900 per call sold ($49 each × 100 = $4,900). Now, let's say the stock is trading at $174 on April 4, 2009 and the calls are selling for $72 each giving an $11,500 loss on the sale of the five calls sold. The stock is up $15,000 (i.e., 500 × $30). If the calls were bought back, thereby liquidating the $11,500 loss, the Straddle Rule precludes deducting the loss in the year of liquidation. The loss, however, can be used to reduce the gain on the offsetting stock position.

So dealings with listed options and traded stock that offset one another is certainly subject to IRS Rule 1092 (unless the calls sold are qualified covered calls as defined in our glossary and at other places) and the selection of an "identified straddle" is one choice available.

The Straddle Rules Section 1092, however, does not address the liquidation of the gain side of the offsetting positions prior to the liquidation of the loss side. So it is assumed that if the gain side is liquidated first, the gain is reported in the year of liquidation regardless of when the offsetting loss position is liquidated, and regardless of how the gain is treated for tax purposes. As you will see, this has interesting implications for ESO hedging and management.

IRS Section 1092 as Applied to ESOs

The application of Rule 1092 to positions where ESOs comprise one side of the offsetting positions is not clear-cut. Although many tax experts claim that the rule does apply, our analysis says that Section 1092 does not apply to offsetting positions where one of the offsetting positions is an ESO (either qualified or nonqualified). The strongest reason for this view is that Section 1092 essentially says that a liquidated loss on one of the offsetting positions must be reduced by the unrecognized gain on the other position. Unrecognized gain in Section 1092 is defined as the gain that would result if the asset were to be sold at its "fair market value." Since ESOs cannot generally be sold to another party, as a matter of contract with the company, there can be no "fair market value" and therefore no unrecognized gain. Since there is no unrecognized gain, then Section 1092 will have no effect even if it did apply. It can also be argued that ESOs have compensation income but no "gain."

Put

A put is a contract that a hedger or speculator enters into with the Options Clearing Corporation whereby the hedger or speculator who owns a put has the right to sell long stock for a specified price throughout a specific period of the option contract to a person randomly selected by the Options Clearing Corporation. This person getting assigned has entered into a contract with the OCC to buy the same amount of stock that the hedger or speculator has the right to sell. The put contract requires the buyer to pay a premium to the OCC which the OCC passes on to the writer of the contract. These contracts trade on various options exchanges around the world.

Call

A call is a contract that a hedger or speculator enters into with the OCC whereby the hedger or speculator has the obligation to sell stock for a specific price throughout a specified period of time to the OCC. The OCC randomly selects a person who has obligated himself to sell stock at a specified price over a specific period of time. These contracts trade on various options exchanges around the world.

Premature Exercise Tax

If a grantee of ESOs owns vested options giving him to the right to purchase 5,000 shares of stock at a price of $20, and the market price of the stock has increased to $40, there would be a gain of $20 on each share of stock. Furthermore, let's say that the ESOs have five years of expected time to expiration remaining. The amount that the grantee would receive upon exercise of the ESOs and subsequent sale of the stock would be $100,000 minus an ordinary income tax liability of 40 percent.

If the Grantee Hedges

If the holder were to hedge (rather than exercise and sell the stock), by selling, for instance, 50 calls on the stock with an exercise price of $40 and having 16 months to expiration, the risk of holding the ESOs is reduced by about 55 to 60 percent. Now assume that the stock then advances in about 12 months to $55, making the subsequent gains on the ESOs reduced by $50,000 from losses on the listed calls sold. These numbers are just estimates. If we wished to be precise we would need precise assumptions about volatility, interest rates, and time remaining.

Assume that the loss on the listed calls sold is $50,000, and they are liquidated. Longer-term calls with a different exercise price could then be sold to maintain a hedge. The Wash Rule would not apply here—see Appendix A. In our view, the $50,000 loss would be ordinary loss if IRS Section 1221 (the IRS hedging transaction statute) applied.

When Section 1221 Does Not Apply

What happens if Section 1221 does not apply when particular ESOs are one of the offsetting positions? If Section 1221 did not apply, then the $50,000 liquidated loss on the calls can be used immediately as an ordinary loss of $3,000 every year or to eliminate other capital gains that the grantee may have or will have in the future. When there is a profit on the calls written or puts bought, capital gains taxes will apply. Selling (writing) calls never creates a long-term capital gain regardless of the period held. The sale is considered closed if the calls are bought back at a profit (or loss) or if the calls are out-of-the-money at expiration. The gain is then reportable as short-term capital gain when closed. If the calls sold are in-the-money when they expire, the listed call owner will exercise, and the writer (i.e., seller) becomes short stock. This is not considered a closing of the written calls but a continuation of the written calls for tax purposes. In other words, it is not a taxable event.

The gain from the selling of the calls, which result in a short position in the stock can be delayed indefinitely as long as the seller of the calls wants to maintain the profitable short position in the stock. If the call writer (now a short seller of stock) closes the short sale with a buy cover order (offsetting or closing out a short stock position), then there is a taxable event. It is either a gain or loss depending on the price paid to cover and the price and terms at which the options were sold.

Buying Puts as a Hedge

If rather than selling calls to hedge, the risk-reducing grantee chooses to buy puts and finds the stock going down substantially after the put purchase, he can sell the puts and achieve a short-term capital gain if the puts are held less than a year or he can achieve a long-term gain if the puts are held over one year. He can also exercise the puts and substitute his long puts for a short stock position. The exercise does not create a taxable event. The gain becomes taxable when the stock is purchased to cover the short stock. This allows the delaying of a taxable event on profits indefinitely until covered.

IRAs and the Straddle

Of course, if the grantee wished to do his hedging inside his individual retirement account (IRA) because he has liquid funds there, his gains will be tax free or tax deferred. How would the losses in an IRA be treated for tax purposes? It depends on whether the straddle rule applied to the purchase of puts to hedge inside of an IRA. Our view is that Section 1092 would not apply unless the assets that were hedged by the purchase of puts in an IRA account are stocks or other traded securities. If this were the case, then the "identified straddle" selection should be made. If the "identified straddle" selection was accepted, then any loss from the purchase of the puts could be used to raise the cost basis of the securities hedged.

IRS Section 1221 deals with situations when hedges are made in the normal course of a business and the gains or losses on the sale of the hedged asset is not a capital asset as defined. If this treatment applied, it would preclude the exposure to the Section 1092 straddle treatment and make it such that all gains and losses on the sales of calls or purchases of puts or short sales of stock would be ordinary gains or losses (unless done inside the umbrella of an IRA).

Fast Fact

IRS Section 1221 deals with situations when hedges are made in the normal course of a business and the hedged assets are not capital assets. Ordinary income taxes apply to gains or losses.

This IRS Section 1221 treatment may apply to nonqualified ESOs, not to qualified ESOs. If the treatment was applied to nonqualified ESOs, we believe that it would have a minor positive impact on hedging ESOs. If a grantee were convinced that there was a good probability that Section 1221 would apply, then he should sell calls, buy puts, or short stock more aggressively.

Wash Sale Section 1091

This rule says that if a trader buys 100 shares of stock at $100 and it goes to $75 and he sells the 100 shares at $75, he cannot deduct the capital loss of $2,500 currently if he purchases 100 shares of the same stock or substantially identical stock or options to buy the stock within 30 days before or after the sale. It also says that if he buys calls at $10 but sells them at $7 and within 30 days of the sale at $7, he buys the same calls, he cannot take the loss currently.

It does not say that he cannot deduct the loss if he buys calls at $10 and sells them at $7 and simultaneously with the sale at $7 he buys longer-terms calls with a higher exercise price. It similarly does not say that the Wash Rule applies to a trader who sells calls at $10 and buys them back at $15 and, within 30 days of the purchase, sells (writes) different calls with higher exercise prices and longer times to expiration.

We are of the view that the Wash Sale Rule will have an incidental impact on hedges against ESOs if any. In fact, the present rule gives us confidence that hedging ESOs with listed calls and puts is tax friendly.

Conclusion

There is some uncertainty as to how taxes will be assessed against calls sold or puts bought to hedge because of the possibility of there being no application of the Straddle Rule and a bit of uncertainty that if the Straddle Rule did apply, whether Section 1221 would make identified straddles unavailable to the nonqualified ESO hedger. But considering all possibilities, hedging ESOs is highly tax friendly. Of course, we can imagine a highly improbable event where the tax treatment for hedging is not favorable.

Example

Assume that a grantee writes calls to buy stock at $60 when she owns the same number of ESOs and the stock quickly goes from $60 to $300. Then there comes a ruling from the IRS saying that the Straddle Rule does not apply to offsetting positions where ESOs are one leg and there is also a ruling that says that IRS Section 1221 does not apply. If the grantee had fully hedged her position and made no delta adjustments as the stock rose, then she would have a concern for this 1-chance-in-100 situation. But we never advise fully hedging the positions. We also advise adjusting deltas along the way if need be. So the 1-shot-in-100 is not something to be concerned with as a practical matter, in our view.

If the grantee/hedger is concerned about 1-in-100 chance events, she should make sure she is always substantially delta long, considering all of her positions. And she certainly should be concerned about holding naked options or naked ESOs, where there is perhaps a 50-in-100 chance of the stock decreasing in price and making the present at-the-money ESOs worthless at expiration.

Example
Selling Apple Computer

Assume that an investor sells ten Apple Computer "naked" listed calls with a strike price of $150 expiring in January 2010 for $46,700 when the stock is trading at $156.34, as was the case on October 1, 2007. These are in-the-money calls. In the first part of the example, in order to keep the example simple, we are assuming that the investor holds no ESOs or stock. Assume also that he holds this position until the listed calls expire. Assume the stock is unchanged at expiration of the calls sold, so the options expire in-the-money. If the stock is unchanged, he will be assigned the exercise notice and will now be short 1,000 shares of stock. Had he covered the sale (i.e., write) of the January 2010 calls right before they expired, he would have a profit of $40,000, which is short-term capital gain when covered. If he buys the stock back at $156.34 immediately after the assignment, again the gain is $40,000, which is short-term capital gain. If he stays short, he will have made the $40,000 without any immediate tax.

If he then buys 13 slightly in-the-money January 2011 listed long-term equity anticipation securities (LEAPS) calls, he still has not created a tax bill. Although his two positions do indeed offset each other, they are not substantially identical for the Constructive Sale Rule to apply. The Straddle Rule Section 1092 would now come into play when the 13 calls are bought.

If the stock goes up substantially after expiration and assignment, the purchase of the stock should be made in order to eliminate the short sale because there is no tax advantage to holding the position. The decision as to whether to hedge the purchase of the stock depends on the grantee's risk attitude. Also, if the investor discovers some other capital losses that can be taken to offset the gain that will result from covering the short sale at a profit, he should take that loss and cover the profitable short sale immediately.

Assume Apple is higher after the sale of calls: If the stock, instead of staying the same after the 2.3 years, traded at $220 at expiration, the written calls would be worth $70,000, giving a $23,300 loss, which can be deducted as a short-term capital loss if covered. If the options are assigned, the investor should buy the short stock back immediately and sell other calls or buy puts if he wishes to remain short deltas.

Instead of selling Apple calls, assume our trader buys at-the-money puts: If the stock goes substantially lower at expiration of the puts, the buyer will have a substantial profit on the puts. He could exercise the puts near expiration and change his long puts into short stock. This is not a taxable event. He could remove most of his profit without having to pay a current tax.

7

Management of ESOs and Premature Exercises

One of the common approaches to managing ESOs that have acquired some intrinsic value is to undertake a premature exercise. Without a hedging plan, which we provide in this book, premature exercise is the only choice available to prevent gains in ESOs from going up in smoke should the underlying stock head south. In this chapter, we present a closer look at the costs of premature exercises, using different assumptions about volatility, prevailing interest rates, and expected time to expiration. As will clearly be seen, the costs of premature exercises are indeed quite high, underscoring the need to develop an alternative plan—hedging with listed options for protecting the value of one's ESOs.

Determining Value

The exhibits in this chapter illustrate how the theoretical values of the ESOs change under different assumptions and stock price movements. These exhibits also illustrate the results of premature exercises when the received stock is sold. We assume that the stock is trading at a price of $20 on the day of the grant. Therefore, the ESOs have an exercise price of $20. Exhibit 7.1 contains the theoretical values for ESOs with these assumed

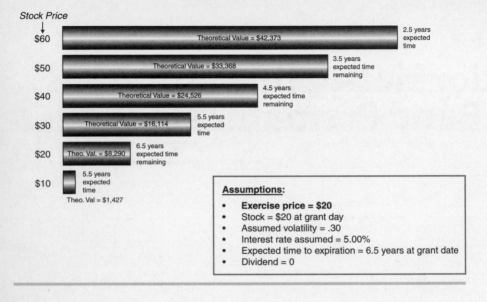

Employee Stock Options Management

Black Scholes Theoretical Value *(1,000 Options)*

Stock Price

$60 — Theoretical Value = $42,373 — 2.5 years expected time

$50 — Theoretical Value = $33,368 — 3.5 years expected time remaining

$40 — Theoretical Value = $24,526 — 4.5 years expected time remaining

$30 — Theoretical Value = $16,114 — 5.5 years expected time

$20 — Theo. Val. = $8,290 — 6.5 years expected time remaining

$10 — 5.5 years expected time — Theo. Val = $1,427

Assumptions:
- **Exercise price = $20**
- Stock = $20 at grant day
- Assumed volatility = .30
- Interest rate assumed = 5.00%
- Expected time to expiration = 6.5 years at grant date
- Dividend = 0

variables. As can be seen, the value depends on expected time to expiration. For example, with 6.5 years expected time to expiration and a volatility assumption of .30, the valuation would be $8,290, which represents pure time premium since the stock price is the same as the exercise price upon granting these ESOs. As the expected time to expiration is shortened and the stock price held fixed, the time premium by definition must drop. The theoretical value, however, rises when the stock price increases. As can be seen in Exhibit 7.1, the theoretical value increases to $24,526 if the price of the stock is $40 based on the assumption of 4.5 years expected time to expiration.

The theoretical value components shift as the price level of the underlying stock price changes, as can be seen Exhibit 7.2. When the price of the stock is $20, the value of the ESOs is equal to its time premium only. There is no intrinsic value since the strike or exercise price is equal to the stock price. But when we assume a price of $40 for the stock, the option has now acquired some intrinsic value, in addition to time

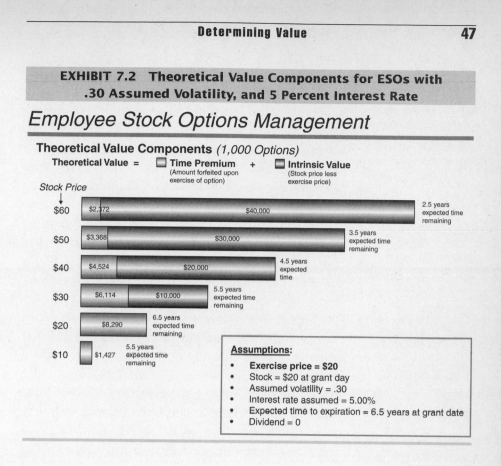

EXHIBIT 7.2 Theoretical Value Components for ESOs with .30 Assumed Volatility, and 5 Percent Interest Rate

premium. The time premium component has dropped to $4,524, and the intrinsic value now stands at $20,000. That is, the options are now $20 in-the-money. This gives the ESOs with a right to buy 1,000 shares at $20, a value totaling $24,524.

The maximum expiration date of the ESOs is ten years from the date of the grant. But we use expected expiration dates since there is a tendency of holders to make premature exercises after the grant day but before expiration, and there is a probability of the employee's not staying with the company for the full ten years, thereby shortening the expected time to expiration. However, if we assume hedging is a choice, many employees would likely hold their ESOs longer, which would alter the equation substantially. However, for now, we will use the aforementioned logic for illustration purposes. The different exhibits in this chapter, therefore, assume that at grant day the expected time to expiration is 6.5 or 6.3 years from the grant day, even though the maximum contractual expiration period could be as long as ten years.

Actual Value of the ESO

The expected time to expiration of ESOs is an artificially shortened option contract life used in valuation models. This idea is based on the assumption that an employee may not stay employed the full life of the option contract and on the probability that he will exercise his options prematurely. The actual value of an ESO, therefore, may be larger if the assumption turns out to be in error and the employee's time of employment is greater than the expected life of the option or he makes no premature exercises.

The assumed volatility and the interest rates are the same in Exhibits 7.1 through 7.3. Each shows .30 volatility with a 5 percent interest rate. All exhibits assume that there are no dividends payable. These first exhibits illustrate how the time premium changes when we change the assumptions about the underlying stock price and expected time to expiration. As can be seen, Exhibits 7.4 and 7.5 show how the time premium changes with the higher assumed volatility. These illustrative ESOs show much higher time premiums. The maximum time premium would be on the grant day when the stock is trading at the exercise price (there is no intrinsic value when the price of the stock is the same as the strike or exercise price). When the ESOs are in-the-money, time premium equals the amount of value that the options have that is above the intrinsic value. The time premium is the amount that is forfeited back to the company when the options are exercised with some time remaining. The darkest areas of the bars in Exhibits 7.3 and 7.6 show the approximate taxes due when the grantee exercises his or her ESOs.

The lightest areas in Exhibit 7.3 show the net after-tax proceeds payable to the grantee upon exercise and sale of the received stock. As can be seen, the net after-tax proceeds are less than half the theoretical value of the ESOs when the stock is trading at the price of $40 and having an expected time to expiration of just 4.5 years. Here, we are assuming that if the employee/grantee exercises his ESOs and then sells the acquired stock when the stock is 100 percent above the exercise price (at $40 when exercise or strike price is $20), the net proceeds ($12,000) after tax would be less than half of the theoretical value ($24,526) of the ESOs prior to the exercise. The theoretical value is the total of all three segments of the bars.

In other words, half of the value of the ESOs is paid out upon exercise in the form of forfeited time premium ($4,526) and an early tax liability ($8,000). The forfeited time premium benefits the employer (a poorly understood concept by most financial advisers).

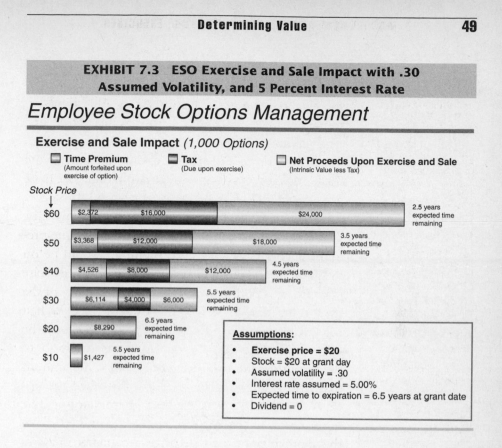

Volatility

If the volatility (assumed here annualized at .30) is far lower , or the time to expiration was much shorter, (translating into lower time premium in the option) the net proceeds from an exercise would approach 60 percent of the theoretical value because the forfeited time premium would be much less. However, if we were to assume higher volatility and a longer time to expiration (such as, say, 8.5 years at grant day), the net proceeds as a percent of theoretical value would fall even lower than 50 percent.

Let's take another example with different assumptions about volatility, interest rates, and expected time to expiration. Exhibits 7.4 through 7.6 assume a level of .60 for annualized volatility, interest rates of 3 percent, and expected time to expiration of slightly less than 6.5—the earlier assumption—to 6.3. Here, we can see that when we change these assumptions, the overall cost from forfeiture of time premium of an early exercise rises significantly.

EXHIBIT 7.4   ESO Theoretical Value with .60 Assumed Volatility, and 3 Percent Interest Rate

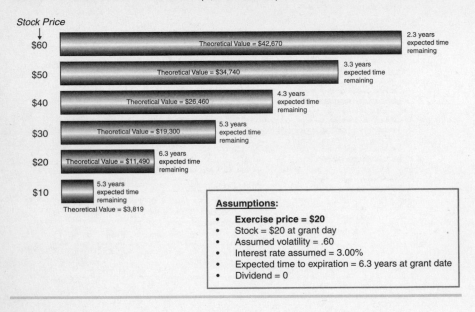

Employee Stock Options Management

Black Scholes Theoretical Value *(1,000 Shares)*

Stock Price

$60 Theoretical Value = $42,670   — 2.3 years expected time remaining

$50 Theoretical Value = $34,740   — 3.3 years expected time remaining

$40 Theoretical Value = $26,460   — 4.3 years expected time remaining

$30 Theoretical Value = $19,300   — 5.3 years expected time remaining

$20 Theoretical Value = $11,490   — 6.3 years expected time remaining

$10 — 5.3 years expected time remaining
Theoretical Value = $3,819

Assumptions:
- **Exercise price = $20**
- Stock = $20 at grant day
- Assumed volatility = .60
- Interest rate assumed = 3.00%
- Expected time to expiration = 6.3 years at grant date
- Dividend = 0

Here again, the maximum contractual expiration date is ten years from the grant day, but the times to expiration are discounted to get the expected time to expiration. At grant day, the assumed expected time to expiration is 6.3 years. The assumed expected dividend is zero in each case. Exhibit 7.4 shows that with the higher assumed volatility there is higher time premium, which can be seen when examining the bar graphs.

Here, the time premium (representing all the value since it is at-the-money) is now $11,490, up from $8,290, despite a slightly less expected time to expiration (6.3 years instead of 6.5) and lower assumed interest rates (3 percent instead of 5 percent). Lower assumed interest rates actually have a lowering effect on an ESO's value, as does shortening the length of time to expiration. But the much higher volatility assumption makes the time premium much larger.

Exhibit 7.5 breaks out the components of value given the changed assumptions. As the reader can see, at a price of $20, all value is time

EXHIBIT 7.5   ESO Theoretical Value Components with .60 Assumed Volatility, and 3 Percent Interest Rate

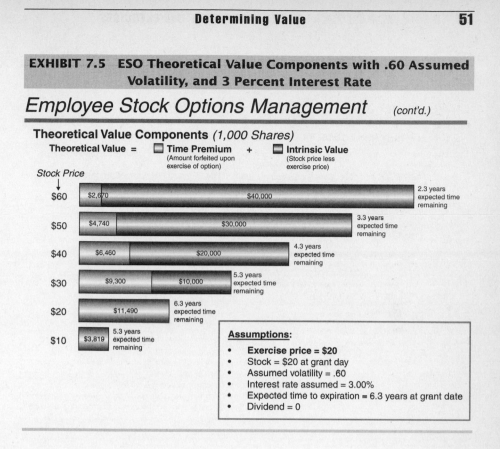

Employee Stock Options Management   *(cont'd.)*

Theoretical Value Components *(1,000 Shares)*

Theoretical Value = ☐ **Time Premium** + ☐ **Intrinsic Value**
(Amount forfeited upon exercise of option) (Stock price less exercise price)

Stock Price

$60 | $2,670 | $40,000 | 2.3 years expected time remaining

$50 | $4,740 | $30,000 | 3.3 years expected time remaining

$40 | $6,460 | $20,000 | 4.3 years expected time remaining

$30 | $9,300 | $10,000 | 5.3 years expected time remaining

$20 | $11,490 | 6.3 years expected time remaining

$10 | $3,819 | 5.3 years expected time remaining

Assumptions:
- **Exercise price = $20**
- Stock = $20 at grant day
- Assumed volatility = .60
- Interest rate assumed = 3.00%
- Expected time to expiration = 6.3 years at grant date
- Dividend = 0

premium, which falls as the price of the stock is higher (deeper in-the-money) and lower (deeper out-of-the-money).

Turning to Exhibit 7.6, the reader can see that a much larger time premium is forfeited upon early exercise of the ESOs with higher levels of volatility. This is so, despite lower interest rates and slightly shorter expected time to expiration. The darker areas in Exhibit 7.6 show the approximate taxes that the executive must pay when the exercise and sale of stock is made at the different price levels (each with an associated time to expiration). The far right side of each bar show net proceeds or the amount that the employee or executive would receive after taxes if he sells the stock or holds on to the stock.

Maximum Time Premium

The maximum time premium of an option is found at-the-money. The deeper in- or out-of-the-money an option, the less time premium it will have. At higher levels of volatility, other things remaining the same, all options will have higher levels of time premium.

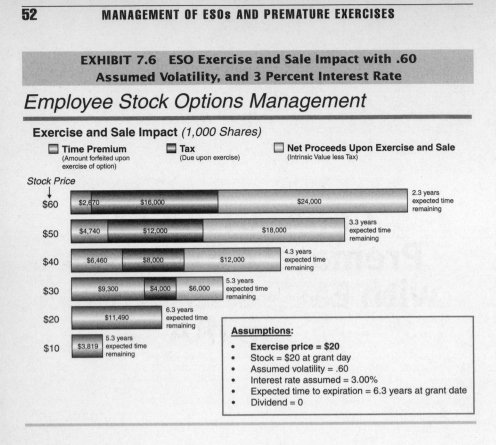

EXHIBIT 7.6 ESO Exercise and Sale Impact with .60
Assumed Volatility, and 3 Percent Interest Rate

Employee Stock Options Management

Exercise and Sale Impact *(1,000 Shares)*

☐ **Time Premium**
(Amount forfeited upon exercise of option)

☐ **Tax**
(Due upon exercise)

☐ **Net Proceeds Upon Exercise and Sale**
(Intrinsic Value less Tax)

Stock Price

$60 | $2,670 | $16,000 | $24,000 | 2.3 years expected time remaining

$50 | $4,740 | $12,000 | $18,000 | 3.3 years expected time remaining

$40 | $6,460 | $8,000 | $12,000 | 4.3 years expected time remaining

$30 | $9,300 | $4,000 | $6,000 | 5.3 years expected time remaining

$20 | $11,490 | 6.3 years expected time remaining

$10 | $3,819 | 5.3 years expected time remaining

Assumptions:
- **Exercise price = $20**
- Stock = $20 at grant day
- Assumed volatility = .60
- Interest rate assumed = 3.00%
- Expected time to expiration = 6.3 years at grant date
- Dividend = 0

Conclusion

If an employee or executive exercises when the stock is 100 percent above the exercise price (i.e., at $40 when strike is $20), he nets just 45 percent of the theoretical value of the options at the higher volatility levels compared with 49 percent when implied volatility is assumed to be at .30. The amount forfeited upon exercise, therefore, has increased from $4,526 to $6,460. Note, however, that the tax burden has remained the same at $8,000 for a premature exercise when the price is at $40 and volatility is at .60 instead of .30. The tax burden is the same because it is based on the amount of intrinsic value acquired in the premature exercise, which is still $20,000. As we have already demonstrated in previous chapters, and will explore in greater depth in subsequent chapters, strategic hedging with listed options can provide a much better outcome for the holder of ESOs, in terms of both a reduced tax burden and forfeiture of less time premium.

Chapter 8

Comparison of Premature Exercises with Early Withdrawal from IRA

In the previous chapter, it was shown how premature exercise carries with it a heavy tax burden and high cost from lost time premium embodied in the ESO. Intrinsic value upon exercise is treated as compensation for holders of nonqualified ESOs, and thus taxed at the detrimental ordinary income rate. This is true regardless of the actions taken following exercise in terms of liquidation of the acquired underlying stock.

We can now further underscore the disadvantages of premature exercise by contrasting the financial choice with another well-known personal finance "no-no"—the individual retirement account (IRA) early withdrawal.

IRA Early Withdrawal

The cost is high in withdrawing from an IRA early, but the short-term needs may outweigh in the typical case. As will be seen in this chapter,

> **Early Withdrawal of IRA**
>
> Liquidating all or a portion of your traditional IRA, which is exempt from taxation for an individual until the age of 70, and thus suffering a tax penalty plus an ordinary income tax on the proceeds from the traditional IRA.

the costs of an early withdrawal from an IRA are actually less than a premature exercise based on a similar assumed sum of money.

Taking the major variables into account (tax rates, IRA and ESO value, and expected time to expiration), the premature liquidating of the traditional IRA has similar penalties compared with the penalties of premature exercises of ESOs and sale of stock. Of course, a lot depends on how much time remains on the options and the level of volatility of the underlying stock, but an option with significant time premium and volatility that is moderate to high, as has been shown, takes a heavy financial toll.

Since no financial adviser would encourage a premature liquidation of a 401(k) plan or IRA, absent an emergency or hardship, why, then, would so many advisers encourage premature liquidations of ESOs? Next, we will show exactly what is wrong with this advice offered by thousands of wealth managers and financial consultants.

An Example of Early Withdrawal

Let's take the example of some hypothetical Google options, which we will assume were granted with the right to buy 1,000 shares of Google stock when the shares were trading at $280 two years prior to vesting. Assume that the grantee believes there is a high probability that he will be at the company for at least five to six more years. And we assume that the present market price of Google is $471 (as it was on May 4, 2007). Assume also that the ESOs had an expected time remaining of 5.5 years with a .30 volatility and a 5 percent interest rate. The theoretical value of these ESOs would be approximately $275,000 based on valuation methods used by financial advisers, as explained in Chapter 3 covering options valuation. That means the intrinsic value would be $191 and the remaining value would be comprised of $84 ($275 − $191 = $84) of time premium per option. If the options are exercised when the stock is at this price after the options vest, the time premium is forfeited back to the company and a current tax of up to 45 percent of the intrinsic value becomes due upon exercise of the ESOs.

Example
Tax Liability Comparison of Traditional IRA Early Withdrawal versus Premature Exercise of ESOs

If the IRA has a value of $275,000, the tax upon early withdrawal, including the penalty, equals $137,500, leaving $137,500 net after tax (assuming a 40 percent marginal tax bracket). For ESOs worth $275,000 (i.e. $191,000 intrinsic value and $84,000 time premium), a premature exercise of ESO results in a tax liability of $76,400. Plus, the grantee forfeits $84,000 time premium or a total reduction of $160,400 from the theoretical value, leaving $114,600 net after tax.

The net result of the premature exercise with sale of stock is $114,600 after tax from options valued at $275,000 pre-exercise, a difference of $160,400, representing a loss of value of that amount. Now let's compare this with a withdrawal from a traditional IRA at age 50, which, remember, is advised only when financial hardship dictates. Assume the value of the assets in an individual investor's IRA equals $275,000. Now if he decides to prematurely withdraw all of the assets, he will pay a 10 percent penalty ($27,500) plus income tax on the $275,000, we'll assume at a 40 percent rate to remain consistent for a comparison with the case of a premature exercise of ESOs used earlier.

This leaves a net tax liability of $137,500, which is greater than the tax liability of the premature exercise. But when we factor in the forfeiture of time premium ($84,000), the premature exercise ends up giving a reduction of $160,400 from the pre-exercise theoretical value. In theory, the $275,000 of value in the IRA is worth a bit more than the $275,000 of theoretical value in the ESOs if the IRA is not disturbed until retirement. This is so because investment gains in an IRA would receive favorable tax treatment and would not have to be liquidated until the investor reaches 70 years old. Even considering the preceding, the comparison still stands as stark evidence of the true cost of premature exercise and what is truly at stake.

Conclusion

Clearly, unless you need to exercise your ESOs prematurely to acquire intrinsic value needed for some financial hardship (there might be other justifications), the best course of action would be to remain in the options to delay paying such a heavy and early tax and forfeiting so much time premium.

By using hedging strategies with listed options—such as selling calls and buying puts (or a combination of the two)—time premium risk can be reduced in addition to tax liability. In the following chapter, we outline the beginnings of a hedging plan and contrast that strategy with prevailing conventional wisdom.

Chapter

9

Strategic Choices for Managing Your ESOs

The strategic choices available to an employee holding employee stock options (ESOs) can be lumped into three categories, the first two traditional approaches: (1) hold options unhedged to expiration (2) execute a premature exercise in whole or part when the options have acquired intrinsic value and (3), when available, hedge with exchange traded options, which is our preferred approach.

Before we turn to the details of how to actually do ESO hedging with exchange traded options in the following chapter, here we take a closer look at the two conventional strategies (holding options unhedged or executing a premature exercise). We look at their major advantages and disadvantages under different sets of assumptions. This chapter provides an explanation of the directional and time premium decay risks of holding unhedged ESOs. Furthermore, the costs of a premature exercise in the form of added tax burden and forfeiture of time premium are examined.

Unhedged Positions Strategy

The equivalent of the "buy and hold" approach in stocks, this do-nothing, unhedged approach offers the most potential gain and the greatest risk. It also offers the least amount of management and accounting costs and

"Naked" ESOs

Naked options are traditionally a reference to a shorting strategy where the trader sells call or put options and collects the premium from the sale. The maximum profit potential is limited to the dollar value of the premium collected minus transaction costs and is realized if the option expires out-of-the money worthless. However, if the market moves the wrong way, there is potential for large losses should the option get in-the-money by expiration. Here, the use of "naked" is broadened to mean having no hedge on ESOs, where you can lose all or part of the intrinsic value and time premium.

required attention time, which may suit persons with just small amounts of ESOs. Unhedged "naked" options are by their nature high-risk speculative instruments. Holding "naked" options, therefore, whether exchange traded or ESOs, is not for the risk averse. The stock may go down, and the time premium will decline even as the stock goes moderately higher.

The choice to simply hold ESOs without exercising makes sense when there is little or no intrinsic value on the ESOs and still a long way to go to expiration.

If an employee/executive fully understands the risks of holding unhedged ESOs, his decision to hold unhedged options to expiration may be the wisest choice. Only time will tell. But it must be pointed out that there is a substantial probability that the ESOs will be worthless on expiration day, especially if the stock is highly volatile. This is the statistical reality, of which few holders of ESOs are aware.

Example

Assume some ESOs have an exercise price of $20 and the stock is trading at $40. Additionally, the ESOs have five years' expected life, and the theoretical value of the ESOs is $25 ($20 intrinsic value + $5 time value). If the holder of ESOs does nothing to hedge the intrinsic and time premium and the stock price is at $60 by expiration, the time premium of the options is zero. There is a gain of $40 of intrinsic value, which would be subject to a compensation income tax, which we assume at 40 percent. On the other hand, if we start with the price of $20 for the stock price, the ESOs may just as likely end up out-of-the-money by expiration as there is a good chance the stock is below $20. Here the value of the ESOs goes to zero. Unhedged ESOs, therefore, have great potential for gain yet about equal potential for loss of their total value.

Premature Exercise with ESO Intrinsic Value

Let's assume that some ESOs have acquired intrinsic value. The employee has waited for the stock to rise, and it did. Now let's say he decides to make a premature exercise when the underlying stock is perhaps 100 percent higher than the exercise price (e.g. stock went from $10 to $20). Assuming for now that part of the proceeds from the sale of the stock is used to pay the exercise price of $10 and any taxes that are due, the ESO holder could then invest the net after-tax proceeds in a diversified portfolio of stocks or mutual funds, as is often recommended by financial advisers and wealth managers.

As we saw in Chapter 7 on the costs and tax implications associated with premature exercise, after-tax results of this strategy can be less than 50 percent of the theoretical (fair) value of the ESOs when the stock is 100 percent above the exercise price.

Of course, if time is running out and the volatility is very low, these may be sufficient reasons to justify such a premature exercise. That is, if the expiration date is very near, there is little time premium remaining on the options, so the cost of premature exercise from the forfeiture of time premium is minimal.

Example

Assume that ESOs, which an employee holds, gives him the right to buy 5,000 shares of stock at $10 per share. If the stock price appreciates to $20 from $10 and he decides to exercise the ESO options, he will have compensation income of $50,000 and a tax of about $20,000. Let's assume that the employee decides to sell some of his acquired stock to pay the exercise price for 5,000 shares and the tax that is withheld. He will then have a highly risky position.

Hedging with Listed Options

Hedging with exchange traded options consists of systematically writing (selling) slightly out-of-the-money long-term calls or buying selected puts versus the ESOs you may hold along with any company stock. This strategy recognizes that there is an advantage to avoiding the forfeiture of remaining time premium and an advantage to delaying taxes, both of which are accomplished by writing slightly out-of-the-money long-term calls alone or in conjunction with the purchase of the company's exchange traded put options.

Which listed calls are the best to write and when should they be sold? The answer depends on a number of factors. Executives who are subject to Section 16(b) of the Securities Exchange Act of 1934 have concerns that other managers do not have. So the exact strategies are somewhat different. However, whether an employee or executive, we generally believe writing long-term, slightly out-of- the-money calls offers the best for all holders of ESOs, a subject we delve into in the following chapter.

Chapter

10

Basic Hedging Strategies Overview

Until now, we have made reference to hedging using exchange traded options and demonstrated why it might make sense to develop and deploy a hedging plan if an employee is a holder of ESOs with or without intrinsic value. Holders of ESOs are likely to have value that represents time premium, as well as possibly intrinsic value. Options that are in-the-money to any extent will have intrinsic value and time premium. Even with no movement of the stock price, the ESO can lose value from time premium decay, a risk known as theta in the options world. In this chapter, call selling is fully explained, with a look at how selling calls can hedge theta and delta risk found in ESO holdings. Additionally, buying puts and shorting stock as hedging tactics are briefly discussed.

Theta and Delta Risk Reduction

As a holder of ESOs, it makes sense to use a hedging strategy, such as selling calls and/or buying puts, that is aimed at reducing risk from theta and delta. Theta risk is exposure to decay of time premium on ESOs and the rate of decay increases as expiration nears. Meanwhile, exposure to delta, or directional risk, can result in loss of an ESO's value as the stock declines.

Fast Fact

The rate of time premium decay increases as the expiration date approaches and thus any time premium in an option will decrease at an ever faster rate going into expiration.

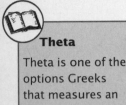

Theta

Theta is one of the options Greeks that measures an option's risk or exposure to time premium decay.

Given the potential for losing value in the ESOs, a grantee should consider whether a hedging plan would meet his financial needs. Before providing examples of how to hedge theta and delta risk, however, we want to explain the workings of the simplest hedging strategies. In this chapter, therefore, we will illustrate exactly what happens when a person wants to write (i.e., sell) exchange traded calls, buy listed puts, or short sell stock regardless of the person's reasons for doing so.

Writing Listed Calls, Buying Listed Puts, or Short Selling Stock

These strategies, as mentioned previously in this book, have become more practical given the dramatic fall in transaction costs and ease of executing options trades with the latest online broker platforms, as well as new regulations that reduce the margin costs for selling options, such as call options.

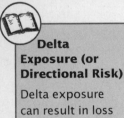

Delta Exposure (or Directional Risk)

Delta exposure can result in loss in an ESO's value. So hedging would offer a potential solution for avoiding reduction in some or all ESO value resulting from decline in the underlying stock price.

Writing Calls to Reduce Delta and Theta Exposure

When a person writes or sells listed call options, he sends an order to an options exchange, done today electronically from an online trading platform, with either a limit order or a market order. In our view, it is best to avoid market orders. The sell order is matched by a buyer of the same calls at the same price the writer is willing to sell. The buyer may have an order to buy at a specific price and if it matches the call seller's sell price, the order is "filled." In other words, the matched prices result in a trade whereby the seller has sold a call, which would be considered an opening position if the seller did not already hold a long call option.

With this type of "agreement" between the two parties, the trades become options contracts with the Options Clearing Corporation (OCC), which guarantees to the buyer the performance and obligation incumbent upon the seller as spelled out in the option contract.

Recall that a seller of a call option is under obligation to deliver stock equal to the obligated shares (100 shares per call option) if the call is exercised and assigned to the seller. The seller of the call then must provide stock to the buyer at the exercise price of the call option. If the seller does not have a long position (i.e., he is a naked call seller), the seller needs to buy stock in the obligated number of shares in the open market and deliver these to fulfill the contract's obligation or he can borrow the stock and remain short stock. If the market price is substantially above the exercise price, this will result in losses. However, many options positions are closed prior to expiration, so assignments can easily be avoided or dealt with. The idea that there could be a penalty from an assignment at expiration or prior is a myth.

The premium or market price of the calls transacted in our hypothetical seller/buyer matching is paid by the buyer to the Options Clearing Corporation, which sends the premium, minus minimal transaction costs, to the seller, who receives the premium into his account with his broker. That premium, plus initial margin in the form of cash or securities, is a good faith deposit into the brokerage account to guarantee performance to the OCC by the seller of the calls. The premium received is the maximum profit that can be made on the sale by the writer or seller of the call options. The brokerage firm will ordinarily pay interest on the proceeds of the sale of the calls and the cash margin deposited. Accounts with cash deposits over $10,000 can have the broker purchase Treasury bills that pay interest on the margin, which is generally a better rate than a broker will pay on cash deposited in an account.

cash or securities, is a good faith deposit into the brokerage account to guarantee performance to the OCC by the seller of the calls. The fact that the OCC acts as the guarantor makes dealing with exchange traded options superior to doing swaps and other derivatives direct with banks and insurance companies.

The initial margin requirements, and the maintenance margin requirements, are substantially less than the margin requirements to short stock, but are not fixed. If the stock advances sufficiently after the sale, the broker could ask for more margin from the option seller, depending on the nature and value of the initial margin deposited. Option positions are marked to market each day so the deposited margin required can rise or fall depending on the movement of the underlying stock and changes in volatility. Obviously, upside moves of the underlying stock will most likely lead to higher maintenance margin requirements, when naked short calls are in the account.

If the seller of the calls, however, holds an equal quantity of stock of the company upon which the calls were sold, then there will be no margin call since the sale of the calls are considered covered by the long stock, assuming there is a match between obligated shares represented by the short calls and long stock shares held in the account. When there is a match between these two assets (short calls and long stock), the upside risk is eliminated since any losses on the calls are more than offset by gains in the long stock. If the call options sold are substantially out-of-the-money, there is potential profit on both the long stock and short calls, thus there is some room for profits from upside directional price gains on the stock.

Fast Fact

Writers of calls create positions by definition that have negative deltas, which can be a hedge against ESOs, which have positive deltas.

Writers (i.e. sellers) of calls create positions by definition that have negative deltas—and therefore potential profit from downside price moves of the underlying stock. The theta value from short calls is positive, which means that time premium erosion accrues to the writer. As we explained above, sellers of calls get the benefit of time premium erosion, which can be used to offset the time premium decay experienced daily by holding ESOs. Selling calls, to be sure, requires no locating and borrowing of stock as would be the case by selling short stock to establish negative deltas.

To provide a simple example of a covered call, let's say that XYZ stock is trading at $100 in March and a long-term call is sold for $20 with a strike price of $100 at-the-money. Assuming the call seller owns the obligated number long stock (100 shares), this is a covered call write. The $20 price of the call is worth $2,000 ($20 × 100 multiplier = $2,000). If the stock expires at $100 or below, the call option becomes worthless at expiration and the seller pockets the full $2,000 as profit.

As long as the stock does not fall more than 20% by expiration of the long term call options (known as a LEAPS option), the seller will make money overall. In other words, if the stock position does not lose more than $2,000, the net result on the covered call write is positive. If the stock drops below $80 a share, however, there will be losses dollar for dollar on the long stock.

Given the same covered write pricing cited above, if the stock settles above $100 at expiration, it is still possible for the call seller to make money on the call itself. Recall that $2,000 was taken in as premium with the sale of the covered call. The good news is that if the stock moves higher, it is impossible to lose money on a covered call write because losses on the short call are exactly offset by gains on the long stock.

While the long stock upside potential is nonexistent, the premium collected from selling the $100 at-the-money call becomes a profit as time premium goes to zero at expiration at any price point. Keep in mind, however, that we are working with an at-the-money call option in this example. It is possible, however, to sell out-of-the-money calls, collect premium, providing some downside protection, and now have upside directional potential. This becomes important in the ESO hedging story, to be addressed in subsequent chapters.

Let's turn now to an actual case involving Google LEAPS calls to illustrate how gains and losses can arise with movement of the underlying stock price. Exhibit 10.1 provides a look at a profit/loss diagram at expiration for the sale of a Google $430 call, having an expiration date in January 2011 with 584 days of time premium.

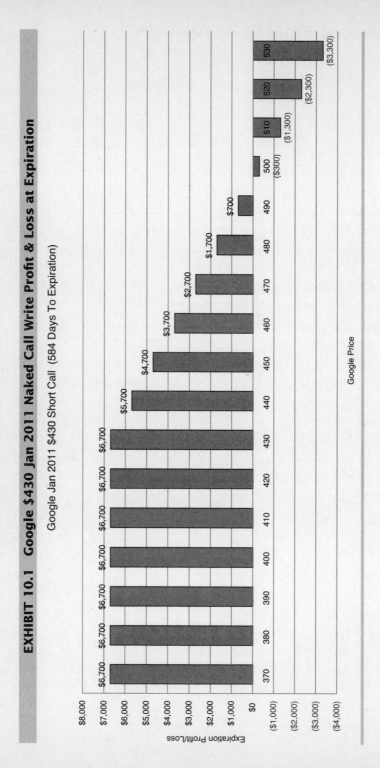

EXHIBIT 10.1   Google $430 Jan 2011 Naked Call Write Profit & Loss at Expiration

Google Jan 2011 $430 Short Call (584 Days To Expiration)

Call Writing Profit/Loss Analysis

As we can see, the premium collected ($6,700) for one Google 2011 call option (representing 100 shares of stock) is the maximum profit that can be gained. But the upside loss potential is unlimited. As can be seen in Exhibit 10.1, the profit level declines at higher price levels, and shows a loss of −$300 if Google closes at a price of $500 on expiration day, losing $1,000 for every $10 move higher by Google beyond $500. For example, as shown in Exhibit 10.1, if the stock price trades higher by expiration to $510, there is total loss of $1300 on the short call, an increase of $1,000 in losses. When the position was opened, the January 2011 $430 call was valued at $67 ($6,700 in time premium was collected) and was slightly out-of-the-money since the stock price was at $416. The options had 584 days remaining until expiration.

Volatility levels were approximately .33, just below average for the past three years for Google. Breakeven for the short call is at the price of $430 plus $67, or $497, and beyond this point there would be losses on a short call if not hedged by ESOs or long stock. At expiration, if the price of the stock is at $430 or lower, the call would expire worthless and the hedger would keep the entire $6,700 of premium collected upfront from the sale of the call as profit. This gain, as we see in Exhibit 10.1, can be a hedge against losses on ESO positions held, either by providing offsets to price declines or time premium decay (or both). Selling calls without any long stock or long calls (such as ESOs), however, is not hedging, and is considered speculative trading.

Exhibit 10.2, provides a look at Google ESOs, granting the right to purchase 100 shares of Google at $320. As can be seen, the upside potential is unlimited, showing an at-expiration profit of $10,000 at a Google stock price of $420 upon expiration. At a price of $420, the ESOs are $100 in-the-money, which represents $10,000 of intrinsic value at expiration ($100 × 100 shares). Therefore, just prior to expiration the ESO holder could exercise the ESOs and acquire 100 shares of Google at $320 and then sell them at $420, representing a taxable gain of $10,000. But what about time premium in the equation? Effectively, it just eroded away because on expiration day there is no more time premium.

For example at $420 the intrinsic value is $10,000 at expiration but the total value has dropped from $15,200 over the 584 days. So there was no increase in value. In fact Google would have to be over $472 to make the ESOs be valued higher than they were 584 days earlier.

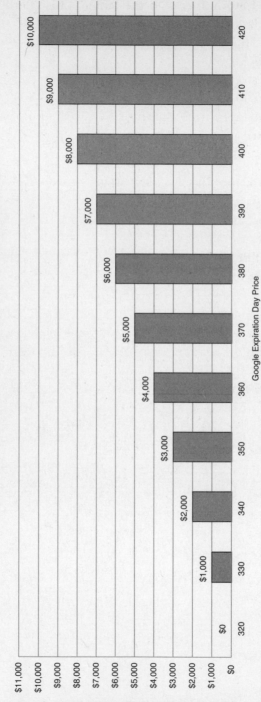

EXHIBIT 10.2 Google $320 ESOs Value at Expiration (Intrinsic Value)

Google $320 Exercise Price ESO (Value At Expiration for 100-Share Equivalent ESO)

Had the ESO holder sold the January 2011 $430 call for $6,700, and the stock landed at $420, he would receive the $10,000 of intrinsic value plus the $6,700, thereby making it such that the value of the ESOs increased from $15,200 to $16,700.

Had the stock landed at $500, the ESOs together with the sale of the call at $6,700 would have achieved a $17,700 value.

The time premium on the ESOs, when there were 584 days remaining until expiration, was $5,200, which is based on a Black-Scholes model valuation with no further discounting for expected time to expiration. The example here again assumes that the ESOs giving the holder the right to buy 100 shares of Google stock was granted at an exercise price of $320 with 584 days to expiration.

On the downside, given a price of Google below $320 at expiration, the entire $15,200 value of the ESOs is lost but there would be a gain of $6,700 on the call sold. By hedging with short calls, however, it is possible to hedge this time premium risk partly or fully, which you can see in Exhibit 10.3. In Exhibit 10.3, it should be made clear, we simplify to a simple one-to-one call sold to ESO equivalent shares, leaving a cap on upside gains. Using deeper out-of-the-money calls, however, allows for much more potential upside, should that be the aim in a hedging plan.

Exhibit 10.3 provides a look at a short Google $430 call having 584 days remaining before expiration combined with the same Google ESOs representing the right to buy 100 shares of Google at $320. As can be seen, in this example, there is no upside risk of loss because the ESOs will provide an offset to any potential losses on short calls.

In Exhibit 10.3 the number of calls sold (one, representing 100 shares of short stock) matches the long shares equivalent positions in the ESOs holding. This means that the ESO hedger is never naked. For margin purposes, a seller of calls may be "naked" in an exchange traded options account, since the holder of ESOs would not be able to

More on Delta

Delta is one of the most important options Greeks—a risk gauge that measures an option's exposure to directional moves of the underlying stock. Delta shows you how much an option's value will increase or decrease from a given move of the underlying stock. Delta risk increases dramatically if the option is near the strike price as the expiration date gets close. Deep-in-the-money options have very large delta risk and deep-out-of-the-money options have just the opposite.

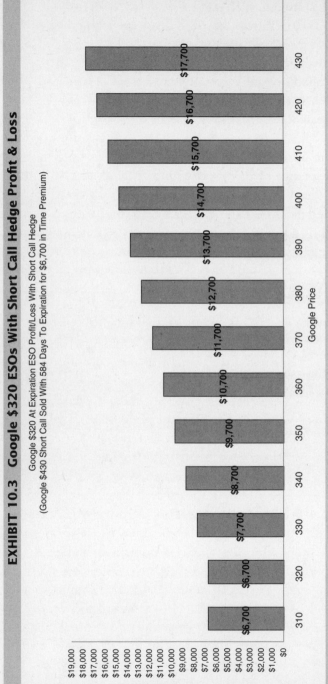

EXHIBIT 10.3 Google $320 ESOs With Short Call Hedge Profit & Loss

Google $320 At Expiration ESO Profit/Loss With Short Call Hedge
(Google $430 Short Call Sold With 584 Days To Expiration for $6,700 in Time Premium)

transfer ESOs to the exchange traded options trading account, a point we return to in subsequent chapters.

Exhibit 10.3 shows the payoff at expiration when a Google listed January 2011 $430 call is sold against Google ESOs presenting the right to buy 100 shares of Google at $320. In traders' lingo, this situation would be called owning a vertical call spread. The positive deltas would be about 30. Note, though, that while the ESO would be worthless at $320, there would actually be a balance of +$6,700 in the hedger's account.

On the upside, increasing net values are realized at expiration in a Google price range of $330 to $430 ($7,700 to $17,700). But any prices above $430 lead to no additional net gains, in this example. If we wish to retain long delta positions, we can do so by buying back a higher delta call and selling a lower delta call. If we had larger positions, we could and should maintain substantial positive delta positions throughout.

Fast Fact

The premium or market price of calls is paid by the buyer to the Options Clearing Corporation, which sends the premium, minus minimal transaction costs, to the writer, who receives the premium into his or her account with a broker.

Finally, to retain a greater potential gain the hedger can purchase listed puts in lieu of call sales, which is not illustrated here but briefly discussed below.

Buying Puts for Downside Protection

When a person buys exchange traded puts, he or she is either speculating on an anticipated downside move or using the long puts to reduce risk by hedging stock or ESOs: The mechanics are similar to selling calls. The difference is that the buyer of the puts pays the premium to the seller of the puts, through the OCC, for the right to sell the stock at a specific price, whereas the writer of the calls receives the premium. The contract becomes one with the OCC, where the rights of the buyer of the puts are guaranteed. The puts are generally paid for in cash, with no need for extra margin to be deposited when adverse moves in the stock price occur.

Puts can never lose more than the premium paid under any circumstances. Buying puts creates negative deltas, positive gammas, and negative thetas (i.e., erosion of premium accrues against the buyer and thus is a significant risk factor). Puts can be bought inside an individual retirement account (IRA), whereas selling unhedged calls is generally not allowed in retirement plans.

Carefully Exercised Puts

As we saw earlier, buying puts offers the potential for the holder of the puts to gain after selling the puts, and be taxed at a long-term capital gains rate if the puts are held for over one year. Buying puts also has the potential for the gains to be untaxed if the buyer carefully exercises the puts and then hedges the short stock position with call purchases.

Short Selling Stock as a Hedge

Selling stock short means the selling of stock that the seller does not own and borrowing someone's stock that is owned and delivering the borrowed shares to the buyer. It is all done by retail traders today with the click of a mouse, assuming the broker with which you have an account has the stocks to sell short, which is usually the case for most well-known stocks. On some occasions, the seller does not borrow and deliver but merely fails to deliver to the buyer. This is referred to as "naked short selling." Some companies prohibit short selling of stock by their employees and the Securities and Exchange Commission (SEC) rules prohibit some executives from short selling stock. While trading in puts and calls is generally allowed, there are SEC restrictions on officers and directors and holders of more than 10 percent of the stock.

Short selling stock potentially allows the gains to not be taxed at all, as can be seen from the following example.

Google Short Sale Example

Assume for a moment that a person wished to short sell 1,000 shares of Google when the stock was trading at $600 per share. The seller would instruct his or her broker to short 1,000 shares at $600. The broker finds a lender of 1,000 Google shares and makes the sale in the marketplace. The $600,000 of sales proceeds are deposited into the brokerage account, which earns interest for the broker. If the short seller is a market maker or large customer, however, the brokerage firm may grant up to 80 percent of the interest to these short sellers.

The fact that the proceeds are not generally available to the average short seller is an incentive to write Google calls and buy puts as a substitute for shorting stock. However, the markets in the stock are generally more efficient than the options. That factor weighs in the direction of shorting stock, unless the execution in the options is efficient or the bearish trader believes the calls or puts are mispriced, allowing him to take advantage of the mispricing. Regardless of these factors, for the retail trader or hedger, in general, it is best to use short calls or long puts for hedging, or a combination of the two strategies, as mentioned previously.

The short seller is required to allow the proceeds of the short sale into his broker's account, plus make a deposit of extra cash or securities equal to $300,000 (for the Google example) to his account to initiate and maintain the short sale (margin deposit). Selling calls and buying puts require less margin per short delta than short sales, especially with the new margin rules in effect as of April 2006 for accounts with $100,000 or more in value.

If the stock fluctuates up after the short sale is made, the short seller's maintenance margin requirement will increase, thus often requiring an additional deposit of cash, a reduction of the short position, or an offsetting transaction. If the stock decreases in value, margin requirements decrease and profits can be removed without tax or borrowing.

If Google went to $400 after the short sale at $600, $200,000 would be transferred to the trader's account from the broker's account, and his margin requirement would be reduced by $100,000. So he could remove $300,000 from his account with no borrowing or taxes.

If the stock then went to $200, he could remove another $300,000 with no borrowing or taxes.

Did You Know?

Short selling stock or call options allows the hedging of ESO risks to efficiently enhance the after-tax results to holders of ESOs. However, selling calls instead of short selling to hedge ESOs is by far the preferred way, in our view. Combinations of call sales and put buys can be the best alternatives.

Of course, if Google stock goes up after the short sale is made, there are transfers of money in the opposite direction and the maintenance margin requirement goes up accordingly. If the short position is covered at a loss, then there is a taxable event (a loss) upon the cover.

Short selling stock or options allows the hedging of ESO risks and enhancing the after-tax results to holders of ESOs. However, selling calls to hedge ESOs is by far the preferred way, in our view, although combinations of call sales and put buys can be attractive alternatives due to tax and margin considerations.

Buying puts also offers more protection from extreme moves on the downside and allows more upside potential gain on the combined positions of long puts and long ESOs.

There is a cost to those advantages of put purchases in that there is erosion of the time premium, which may result in the stock's moving somewhat lower and the puts not increasing. Generally, out-of-the-money puts are the most overpriced exchange traded options that are traded. So, if those are bought, there is another extra cost. We would advise staying away from doing "collars" because of the mispricing of the puts and calls.

Chapter

Constraints on Hedging
Real and Imagined

B ased on the advice dispensed by financial planners and advisers with a specialty in ESO management, it would seem that they possess little, if any, experience trading stock options as a member of an exchange or as a manager of portfolios containing equities and derivatives. Therefore, for most in the industry, their perspective is quite different from the vantage point of a professional trader.

Probably due to a combination of self-interest and lack of expertise, most industry professionals will discourage ESO holders from pursuing a hedging approach to management of the risk and potential reward, usually objecting to hedging using one or more of the objections listed here:

- There are prohibitions in options plans or award agreements.
- Hedging defeats the purpose of the grants by reducing alignment of interests.
- Large amounts of margin are required to hedge.
- There are SEC constraints on hedging for Section 16 executives.
- Tax constraints, including the mismatching of tax treatments apply.
- The Straddle Rule and the Constructive Sale Rule constrain hedging.

- Large transaction costs are associated with hedging.
- There is a possible violation of the blackout periods due to early assignment.
- Hedging is too complicated.

These objections notwithstanding, this book provides the necessary antidote to what in our opinion is an industry simply not providing clients with a full range of choices. When they claim that there are significant "constraints" on hedging for employees and executives, in our view, they are overstating the case. This chapter provides, in particular, answers to, and explanations of, these so-called constraints.

The Case against Hedging

Alignment of Interests

This refers to the fact that an employee who holds ESOs, will generally benefit when the company stock rises. He would have a common interest with the shareholders in seeing this happen since both the employee and the stockholders stand to benefit. Liquidations of ESOs by exercise and sale of stock is not traditionally viewed as delinking this alignment, while hedging, even partially, is considered by some as a dismantling of the alignment.

In our opinion, all of these so-called constraints taken together do not amount to what could be considered significant constraints on hedging. That is, in general there is no significant obstacle to hedging effectively. In fact, in a paper published in March 2000 in the *Columbia Law Review,* David Schizer, now dean of Columbia Law School, unsuccessfully attempts to make a case against hedging employee and executive stock options. We recommend that it be read.

In his paper entitled "Executives and Hedging: The Fragile Foundation of Incentive Compatibility," Professor Schizer makes several claims that we agree with and a few that we disagree with. For example, he claims that the Constructive Sale Rule (Internal Revenue Code Section 1259) generally will not apply when hedges are made, a conclusion with which we concur. However, he claims that the IRS Straddle Rule (Section 1092) will apply. We are of the opinion that hedging by selling calls and buying puts versus ESOs will not create a Section 1092 straddle.

Schizer attempts to undermine the hedging argument by claiming that it defeats the alignment of interests between employee and executive and the company. He suggests that employee and executive premature exercises and stock sales do not eliminate alignment as much as hedging. Interestingly, he does agree that premature exercises do forfeit time premium, and that such an action incurs a premature tax. He does conclude, notably, that in most cases hedging is not prohibited by the company. He gives no indication, however, that he understands the risks associated with holding naked ESOs or other equity compensation and offers no remedy.

Are There Prohibitions on Hedging by the Company?

Companies seldom impose a complete ban on using options to hedge the risks of holding ESO grants. But there are cases of companies that believe hedging defeats the purpose of the ESO grant. Allegedly, these companies want to forge an alignment of interests. Banning any hedging strategies essentially restricts the choices of ESO employees and reduces the real and perceived value of the ESOs to the holders.

Fast Fact

Companies seldom impose a complete ban on using options to hedge the risks of holding ESO grants. They do ban transfers and pledges of ESOs.

Even if the company bans hedging using the company's stock or stock options, an employee can hedge by writing calls on a competitor's stock or of several other companies whose stock price is positively correlated with the employer stock. This can achieve a reasonable hedge in most circumstances.

There are some who claim executives from Goldman Sachs and J.P. Morgan shorted Bear Stearns, Lehman Bros, and Merrill as a strategy of hedging their own equity compensation positions.

Those same companies, which either ban or discourage hedging, allow and sometimes encourage the premature exercise of ESOs and sale of stock, which reduces the alignment of interests much more than hedging the ESOs. Of course, it also improves the company's bottom line, which they might claim realigns the interests, but at the expense of the employee. The Google transferables, for example, invite early exercises. But few criticize the Google transferables as reducing the alignment of interests.

But the premature exercise would completely sever the alignment, so you cannot have your cake and eat it too, which seems to be what companies and many financial planners would like. What sensible and rational person would argue that an employee who does not own ESOs or stock, after a premature exercise and sale, has a greater alignment of interests than an employee who owns substantially in-the-money ESOs and has written some out-of-the-money long-term calls? None. But that is exactly what the design of some plans assumes when restricting hedging. We make no such assumption.

To the contrary, hedging actually does not defeat the purpose of the options plan. Our belief is that a properly designed and administered company options plan will align interests, especially one that considers the employee interests and prohibits executive abuses. Hedging, although reducing risk, does not defeat the ostensible purpose of the grant to foster alignment. Hedging, in fact, can preserve alignment for a longer period of time. Finally, it is the only strategy of managing ESOs that offers an efficient exit of the options positions, while preserving alignment of interests.

Tip

Despite claims to the contrary, most companies do not generally ban or restrict ESO hedging with listed options. Even where ESO hedging is prohibited in the options plan, it would be possible to use stock options of a highly correlated competitor stock to hedge, even if not a perfect vehicle.

Are Margin Costs Prohibitive?

Are there large amounts of margin required to hedge options? Not really. Writing "naked" calls requires margin to be deposited in the form of cash or securities. Using the Chicago Board Options Exchange (CBOE) page as a guide, we find the following minimum requirements for various positions:

Example

To calculate how much Regulation T margin would be required to hedge an option position, you can use the margin calculator at the CBOE web site. See www.cboe.com/tradtool/.

To calculate customer portfolio margin (CPM) minimums, available with $100,000 or more in an account, go to the following page: https://cpm.theocc.com/tims_online.htm

Example
Margin Calculation for Short Call
(Regulation T Strategy-Based Margin)

To calculate the margin required to sell a January 2011 call with a strike price of $110 when the stock is trading at $100 take the greater of the two values generated by the following rules (in the following case, they give the same results):

1. One hundred percent of option proceeds, plus 20 percent of underlying security value less the out-of-the-money amount, if any.

2. One hundred percent of option proceeds plus 10 percent of the underlying security value.

Thus the initial minimum margin requirement to sell one AAPL call with a strike price of $190 when the stock was trading at $160 is 10 percent of the underlying stock value or $1600.

For additional strategies and margin requirement examples for a stock trading at $100, the following requirements would apply as presented in Exhibit 11.1. As can be seen, when the strike is $110 for a price of $100 on the underlying, the margin required is $1000.

Many holders of ESOs also own stock of the company. This generally allows the writing of "qualified covered calls" and up to twice as many out-of-the money naked calls, with no margin requirement. In fact, if an optionee owns stock, he may remove most of the proceeds of the "writes" from his brokerage account whether covered or naked. If the employee owns stock in a retirement account or an IRA, it is possible to write covered calls in those accounts. Similarly, there would be no margin requirement in such accounts.

EXHIBIT 11.1	Regulation T Margin Requirements	
Position Description	Initial Margin Required	Maintenance Margin
Short call exercise. pr. $110	$1,000 = 10% of $10,000	$1,000
Short call exercise. pr. $100	$2,000 = 20% of $10,000	$2,000
Collar $110 exercise. pr. of puts × $95 ex. pr. Plus margin for the call sold.	$1,000 plus price of put	$1,000
Purchase put ex. pr. $95	Price of put = $1,130	None

Note: Assumes 2 years to expiration, and .30 volatility and a stock value of $100.
Source: CBOE

Did You Know?

Margin requirements are required to be posted in any trading account when selling calls. However, new margin rules have lowered requirements for calls sold short without any underlying hedge in the account. These new margin requirements are based on a risk-based assessment known as customer portfolio margin, or CPM, and it became available to the retail trader in April 2006.

Whether operating under CPM or strategy-based margin rules (Regulation T), any calls that are considered naked (not hedged by other options or long stock) by the brokerage firm could lead to a margin call if the stock increases enough. However, margin calls (meaning the account value is not sufficient to meet margin requirements) could be dealt with easily and efficiently by buying back some of the shorted naked calls or exercising prematurely a small portion of the ESOs, and then either selling the stock or holding the stock in a margin account. Of course, if proceeds of the sale were removed, those could be returned to cover any margin requirements.

Are There Securities Laws or SEC Rules that Constrain Hedging?

Sections 16(b) and 16(c) of the Securities Exchange Act of 1934 apply only to officers, directors, and owners of 10 percent or more of company equity. Securities and Exchange Commission (SEC) Rule 10b(5), however, applies to all buyers and sellers of securities. Section 16(b) of the Act declares that any profits made by officers, directors, and owners of 10 percent or more of the stock as a result of trades of equity securities within six months of acquisition are recoverable by the company. Since we advise ESO holders to hedge by writing long-term listed calls, officers, directors and owners who fall into Section 16(b) should not run into a problem with this section of the statute because they would not have to prematurely close profitable positions, or have any options expire inside the six-month window.

However, the ESO holder should be very conscious of 16(b) when making any trades within six months of each other. Some claim that grants of ESOs are exempt from inclusion in the scope of 16(b), but we are not sure of that exemption. It is best to assume that 16(b) applies unless a stronger precedent is established legally with specific cases. We believe that a strong case may be made that many ESO grants are not exempt, although it seems that courts do accommodate the executive optionee on that issue.

Section 16(c) and Rule 16c(4) make it illegal for executives to short sell their company's stock or stock options. However, the sale of calls is permitted to the extent that the seller holds offsetting stock or substantially in-the-money ESOs (i.e. if the calls sold are out-of-the-money).

There is a private letter ruling from the SEC by Anne Krauskopf of the Office of Chief Counsel of the SEC to Credit Swiss First Boston (CSFB) dated March 18, 2004. This letter from the SEC Office of Chief Counsel is in response to a request from CSFB to the SEC Division of Corporate Finance to comment on a package of trades to be made by CSFB with some of its clients. The request is for a holder of substantially in-the-money, vested, nonrevocable ESOs to be allowed to do the following trades and be in compliance with SEC Rule 16c(4).

Those trades were to (1) sell out-of-the-money calls and (2) buy out-of-the-money puts, and (3) sell other puts with the same exercise price and expiration date as the ESOs (these would be puts that are substantially out-of-the-money). The sale of out-of-the-money calls and the buying of out-of-the-money puts is generally called a collar. The SEC agreed that the three trades, together with the holding of substantially in-the-money, vested ESOs, were consistent with SEC Rule 16c(4).

Viewed differently, the four positions consisted of a long vertical call spread (in exchange lingo) and a long vertical put spread. Synthetically, the position is net long the underlying stock. Done together, long in-the-money ESO calls and short out-of-the money calls combined with long out-of-the-money puts and short further-out-of-the-money puts, would thus be slightly bullish on balance. If the put positions were

Margin Call
Request by a broker to bring an account back in line with required margin levels. Typically, an adverse move of the underlying might push the value of the account lower and, at the same time, cause the margin requirements to increase. If the account value is below the maintenance level for margin (the minimum amount of value needed in the account for margin), the trader must add new funds or reduce position risk, or both. Generally, it is easy to manage a margin call simply by adjusting an option position, such as buying back short calls, to reduce the margin requirements or doing margin reducing spreads.

eliminated, the remaining position would be even more bullish. When we explained to Anne Krauskopf the nature of the CSFB positions, she agreed that the elimination of the put vertical spread would be more bullish, thereby complying with SEC Rule 16c(4).

Therefore, if an executive owns substantially in-the-money vested ESOs and writes out-of-the-money calls, he should not be in violation of 16c(4). If he does a collar against the same in-the-money ESOs without the sale of the extra put (thus turning the overall position possibly short the stock), he would in violation of 16c(4). SEC Rule 10b(5), meanwhile, should not be a problem to comply with in hedging ESOs with listed calls any more than Rule10b(5) represents a problem to comply with when trading stocks. Rule 10b(5) prohibits the trading of securities based on nonpublic material information.

Tax Implications as Constraints

Are there tax restraints, including the possible mismatching of gains and losses, that make hedging risky? Some critics of hedging with listed calls and put options would say yes, and they attempt to demonstrate why with the use of "straw man" cases, which they then proceed to shoot down. Here's one such scenario often trotted out by those arguing against hedging. Suppose a stock is trading at $10 and an employee owns ESOs to buy 1,000 shares of stock at $10. This means the ESO has only time premium, therefore no intrinsic value (it is not in-the-money and instead is at-the-money).

The argument then proceeds by making the assumption that the employee writes (sells) ten listed calls with a strike price of $10 against the ESOs, representing 1,000 shares of stock. The next step then involves assuming the stock increases substantially to $100 (+900 percent), making it such that the employee has a large loss on the written calls and a large gain on the ESOs (let's say perhaps an $87,000 loss on the calls and a $90,000 gain on the ESOs, since the net deltas will be long in the early stage of the position). Since the claim is that the loss will probably be a short-term capital loss and the intrinsic value in the ESOs will be considered compensation income, the tax treatments will be mismatched. The after-tax results will be as shown in Exhibit 11.2 if the mismatching occurs that critics suggest but that we disagree with.

EXHIBIT 11.2 After-Tax Results if Mismatching Occurs	
Ordinary Income from the ESO	$90,000
Ordinary tax at a 40% rate	$36,000
Capital loss on the call writes	-$87,000
Tax credits from capital loss	$1,200 per year*
Capital tax loss carry forward after year one	$84,000
Total current loss after tax	-$34,800

*Recoverable yearly at $1,200 per year. However, this result assumes that the positions are fully hedged to start and that no adjustments are made along the way. It also assumes that IRS Section 1.1221 does not apply.

That certainly is not a good result. But what is the probability of a stock's being above $100 when it started at $10 perhaps six years ago? The chance is about 1 in 300 for a stock with a .30 volatility. These critics use a 1-in-300 shot to criticize the hedging strategy (and assume aggressive call writing). If they used a $10-to-$40 price range, the chance is still a 1-in-33 shot. Regardless, we do not advise selling at-the-money calls on 100 percent of the ESOs partly for this reason. We advise writing slightly out-of-the-money calls against in-the-money ESOs and often advise writing calls on only 50 to 70 percent of the total ESOs owned. This leaves significantly long delta in the position for upside gains. And we timely adjust the option position deltas along the way to be always substantially long deltas.

So the mismatched tax treatment objection is not really one at all. In fact, as an objection it is not realistic, and probably reveals more about the lack of understanding by industry professionals of hedging strategies than it does about the viability of hedging. The well-informed hedger knows that hedging is highly tax friendly, as we demonstrate elsewhere in this book.

For example, the gains or losses from the writing of calls against non-qualified ESOs would probably be ordinary gain or loss, if IRS Section 1221 was relied upon and the "hedging transaction" was designated as a 1221 "hedging transaction." If the designation of a "hedging transaction" was not accepted by the IRS, the gain or loss would be short term capital gain or loss. If there are other capital tax losses to be used against those gains, then there could be no tax at all on the profit from the written calls. If long-term puts are bought and become profitable, the gain could be long-term capital gain. We are of the opinion that the IRS Section 1092 Straddle Rule does not apply to hedging versus ESOs whether they are qualified or nonqualified. In view of all factors, hedging by writing calls and buying puts against ESOs can raise the after-tax results considerably.

Straddle Rule and Constructive Sale Rule　As we have talked about in earlier chapters, these rules will have just a very small impact if the hedging of ESOs and stock is done correctly. If by some chance the Straddle Rule IRS Section 1092 would apply to selling listed calls or buying puts to hedge ESOs, the grantee may be able to designate the two positions as an "identified straddle" with some very good tax results.

Are There Large Transaction Costs with Hedging?

Hedging ESOs by writing listed calls can be done for as little as 70 cents per contract. With some companies, the cost of selling 100 listed options contracts (i.e., contacts to buy 10,000 shares of stock) is $70 in total online. The revolution in the broker world and the advent of internet trading has driven down commissions and fees dramatically. The best executions and true experts managing your positions will cost more, of course, but even with additional costs for expert advice the hedger would come out way ahead. The days of onerous commission charges are over, and numerous brokerages exist online with all the tools needed to open an account and begin hedging those ESOs.

Is Hedging Too Complicated?

It's true that hedging is more complicated than the strategy of premature exercise and selling. But it's a lot less complicated once the employee studies this book and learns a little bit more about listed options and how to execute strategies like covered calls and long puts, which are featured in this book. These are beginner-level strategies, so it should not take too much studying to get up to speed with the basic concepts and application of the strategies.

Here is what should be done to get started. Find a broker who will allow the selling of naked calls for the minimum margin requirements determined by the CBOE (ideally portfolio margin instead of strategy based margins). Most brokers will not assist you for various reasons. But there are some very good brokerage firms that want your business. When the appropriate broker is found, deposit any shares of stock or cash and open a margin account. You are now ready to sell "qualified covered calls" and naked calls and buy puts as appropriate. Locate the calls with the longest time remaining that are slightly out-of-the-money that have bid and ask prices that are not too wide. If, for example, the market is $5 bid at $5.20, that's a pretty good spread.

> **Limit Orders**
> A limit order is used to sell or buy an option with a price specified in the order. The broker must fill the trade with the price specified or better, but not less. Always use a limit order when trading options—never use a market order.

If the market is $5 bid at $5.20, place a limit order to sell calls at $5.10 and leave it in the market working. If the stock moves a bit higher, it should get filled, but the hedger can also raise the asking price if he has not gotten a fill. Much can be saved by avoiding market orders when writing calls. Always use limit orders or "not held" or "scale up" sell orders if the broker allows such orders. When the order is filled, tell the broker to send the proceeds immediately, if there is excess collateral in the account.

After the stock moves around and time has passed, there are generally adjustments to be made that will require an understanding of many of the concepts incorporated herein. Later chapters will give some examples of how those adjustments can be efficiently made.

Premature Exercise
Pros and Cons

To any informed trader of stock options, it is nearly always a sin to prematurely exercise exchange traded call stock options. This is because upon exercise, all remaining time premium is forfeited to the writer of the calls. This is great for the seller who normally has to wait until expiration to pocket the full time premium as profit.

With regard to prematurely exercising ESOs, the action can be charterized as a mortal sin.

If the ESOs are prematurely exercised, the grantee does not just lose all remaining time premium, he also will have an early tax. Avoiding Premature Exercises is the cardinal rule in ESO management.

As we explained previously, the tax upon exercise is ordinary compensation income tax on the intrinsic value of the nonqualified ESOs at the date of exercise. The compensation tax upon exercise of ESOs will approach nearly 55 percent of the intrinsic value for California Residents. If the ESOs are qualified (i.e., incentive stock options [ISOs]), then the income may be long-term capital gain on the date of sale of the stock assuming that the stock is held long enough to satisfy a designated holding period to qualify for this tax treatment. Obviously, employees would prefer to receive ISOs, since they would not be taxed on the intrinsic value at the higher rate associated with compensation income tax and

---

Did You Know?

Even if an employee thinks he has ISOs (i.e. qualified options), he may be wrong.

If he is not an employee, he cannot own ISOs. If he does not receive a paycheck with withholding, he is not considered an employee and thus would not be able to receive ISOs.

---

they are eligible for long-term capital gains tax rates, which are the most desirable when taxation is under consideration.

If an owner of ESOs assumes hedging is not a reasonable choice because of company prohibitions, then premature exercise becomes a way for managing risk. Let's take a closer look at why and when a holder of an ESO might chose the premature exercise route, and what costs are involved.

Cashless Exercise

This is the simultaneous buying of the stock at the exercise price and sale of the stock at the market without having to come up with the cash to do so. This can sometimes be done through the company or employer who granted the options, who may have an arrangement with a broker to provide the short-term financing. There are no tax advantages to doing this type of exercise and you will still have to pay withholding out of the sale, and of course any additional brokerage commissions or fees.

Early Exercise with High Costs

If the grantee does not want to hedge or cannot hedge, premature exercises may be the right thing to do to reduce risk and take profits, especially if he places a high value on the cash liquidity.

It is also a simple strategy. There is no rocket science required, even though hedging hardly would require a PhD in mathematics or economics.

Assuming the ESOs have vested and that part of them or all of them are eligible for exercise, the decision to exercise should be guided by some basic principles. The first consideration should be: What is the value trade-off? In other words, if ESOs have vested and are eligible for exercise, and they are in-the-money, first determine how much intrinsic value there is relative to time premium. Let's say that there is $40,000 of intrinsic value and $20,000 of time premium with five years to expiration.

Should a grantee exercise the options to get the stock and liquidate the stock for $40,000 if he at the same time will forfeit $20,000 in time premium?

Probably not, especially given a tax rate as high as 50 percent applied to the $40,000 gain (as much as $20,000). But there may be extenuating circumstances that warrant such a move. Keep in mind that the $40,000 in value is treated as compensation and taxed at ordinary income tax rates, which in the case here we assume to be 44 percent in the future with the current Obama administration. This is true even if the employee holds the stock after exercise and does not sell.

While any gains on the stock (if held for at least an additional year) would be treated as long-term capital gains, the immediate gain from exercise of the options has a large tax consequence. Holding the options, assuming the stock continues to appreciate, however, allows the employee to gain value without having to pay tax. So the trade-off is a big tax bite and lost time premium versus holding the ESOs. Perhaps the employee does not have the cash to acquire the stock at the exercise price. Today, many companies offer the cashless exercise options, whereby the employee is given a short-term loan between exercise and selling the stock.

Tip

When a grantee exercises his ESOs, he has to pay the exercise price of the options, which requires a cash outlay. It is possible to do this without any cash outlay through what is called a cashless exercise. Cashless exercises are increasingly offered by companies to their employees holding ESOs, enabling them to acquire the company's stock and then repay the financing of the exercise through partial or full sale of the stock acquired in the exercise.

Example
How to Exercise an Option

First determine when the ESOs can be exercised by reading the stock option plan and options agreement. It may indicate partial exercise is allowed across time. The employee must inform his company in writing that he intends to exercise the options, stating the specific ESOs he wishes to exercise. There typically is a payment required for the cost of the stock to be acquired, but alternative plans have become available to employees and executives interested in exercising their ESOs.

Chapter

Putting It All Together
The 7 Percent Solution

I n this chapter we demonstrate how to create a simple plan whereby the employee can manage his options positions in a highly efficient and orderly manner. Efficient is defined as maximizing the value of the ESOs to the employee through capture of intrinsic value and time premium.

Fast Fact

Maximize the value of your ESOs by capturing their intrinsic value and time premium.

The plan aims for an orderly reduction of the employee's risk throughout the life of the options and minimizing the taxes otherwise payable by the grantee (also known as the optionee). Finally, the plan aims to help the employer accomplish the objectives of the options plan by maintaining the alignment of employee interests with the employer's interests throughout the life of the options.

The Industry Falls Short in Optimal Management Planning

> **Efficient Management of ESOs**
>
> Efficient management of ESOs is the primary objective of this book. When an optionee manages his or her ESOs efficiently, they are maximizing the capture of time premium and intrinsic value of the ESOs while minimizing the risk and tax liabilities. By avoiding premature exercise through proper hedging, the opportunity costs are reduced and the net gains are increased.

Stock options are still the largest element of equity compensation. Some contend that as many as 11 million U.S. employees own stock options on their employer's stock. In addition, ESOs are granted to millions of employees in China, Russia, Malaysia, Europe, Japan, Canada, India, Great Britain, Australia, and others. A whole industry has grown up around ESOs and related equity compensation plans. Organizations such as the National Association of Stock Plan Professionals (NASPP), the National Committee for Employee Ownership (NCEO), the International Employee Stock Options Coalition (IESOC), the Global Equity Organization, the Coalition to Preserve and Protect Stock Options, the Foundation for Enterprise Development, the Employee Stock Options Advisory Association (ESOAA), the ESOP Association of Canada, and others have been created to deal with the design, installation, and administration of these stock option plans. Some of these organizations offer tax advice on how to handle the options once received.

The members of these organizations are mostly tax lawyers, accountants, human resources personnel, compensation consultants, a few account executives, financial advisers, and marketing personnel.

One area that some of these professionals know is the basic tax treatments of ESOs, ESO plans, restricted stock, retirement plans, and so on. They generally know how to design and efficiently administer those plans, hoping to achieve the objectives of the employer and avoid costly employment litigation.

Some know the complicated pros and cons of expensing options for financial accounting purposes. Some even have a working understanding of the theoretical options pricing concepts.

Few plans are designed with the grantees as the primary concern. Those administrators are also required to explain to the employees what the plans and the options are all about.

There is one area, however, into which only a few will venture. That is into the area of how an employee should manage his or her ESOs, once granted. If an adviser claims to have expertise, he usually advises some form of systematic premature exercise of the ESOs with the immediate sale of some or all of the stock. The employee is then advised to use the proceeds to diversify the employee's investments.

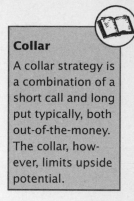

Collar
A collar strategy is a combination of a short call and long put typically, both out-of-the-money. The collar, however, limits upside potential.

Some might even promote the purchase of listed puts or "collars" to hedge the stock received after exercise, especially when the ESOs are qualified. A few promote the buying of puts to supposedly reduce the risk prior to exercising the options. The idea of selling listed call options to hedge those employee stock options, prior to exercise, however, is virtually taboo. Why is that the case?

The reason is that there are very few people in any of those organizations who have had substantial experience trading or managing portfolios containing listed stock options. They are afraid of this terrain because they do not know it well and are not interested in considering the alternative strategies outlined in this book, which often contradict what they believe. Furthermore, they may fear the liability from offering misinformed advice since they are not fully qualified.

Professional option writers, meanwhile, are persons who have extensive experience trading and managing listed options. The authors fall into this camp. We present a hedging approach to managing ESOs from the viewpoint of having personally traded and managed listed options portfolios over long periods. Our strategy will generally far outperform any strategy offered by those advising a system of premature exercises as a management and ESO exit strategy.

Getting Started with a Hedging Plan

Before proceeding with proper management strategies, the employee must understand the details of his employee options award agreement and the company stock plan. All practitioners, regardless of their methods or advice, agree on this point. Therefore, the following steps should be taken to gather necessary information before beginning any hedging.

> **Holding Period**
>
> Holding period typically refers to the length of time the stock is held after being acquired during an exercise of ESOs. Holding periods are usually viewed as either short term or long term for tax purposes. When a holding period is greater than one year plus one day, the stock is considered long term, thus qualifying for preferential tax treatment rates.

1. Know the exact number of options that have been granted and that are still being held. This will indicate the equivalent stock position that an employee holds.

2. Know the exact exercise prices and expiration dates of all the options grants that are still held. The grantee will need this information to determine how to best capture the maximum time premium.

3. Know the vesting periods and penalties for early termination after vesting. This will tell how much would be lost if and when the grantee terminates employment (or is terminated) and help to take actions that can reduce the financial impact.

4. Consider the likely length of time of employment with the company. The expected longevity helps determine the value of the options. Obviously, if the grantee is 100 percent sure he will be staying with the company for the entire period of the option's life, this will impact the valuation of the options held. Although a grantee can never be 100 percent sure, this factor is important.

5. Keep track of any capital losses on stocks or listed options that may be held. These can be used to reduce short-term capital gains from listed options sold, such as short calls which were used in construction of hedges for ESOs.

6. Be aware of any recent capital gains and losses on both stocks or listed options that have been liquidated. Capital losses can be used to reduce short-term capital gains from the sale of listed options which the optionee may have used to hedge against ESOs or restricted stock.

7. Understand whether the options are qualified or nonqualified options. This helps with taxes and applying the correct hedging strategies.

8. Understand the tax treatments of the options upon exercise and sale of stock.

9. Anticipate whether more ESOs will be granted in the future. This will help plan for risk reduction and management of all ESOs and stock.

10. Understand and value the stock positions that are owned outright or in retirement plans or trusts.

11. Know what portion of the entire estate is invested in employer equities. Be thinking about diversity after the employee options are exercised.

12. Understand whether hedging is allowed by the employer for risk reduction and taking profits. If hedging ESOs is prohibited, choices will become severely limited. The strategy would be different since the employee may not even be allowed to write listed calls or buy listed puts on the employer stock.

13. Officers or directors must know how Section 16b of the Securities Exchange Act of 1934 and Securities and Exchange Commission (SEC) Rule 16b(3) applies to them as a grantee of ESOs. Section 16c and SEC Rule 16c(4) also apply, so executives should thoroughly familiarize themselves with these rules.

Additional essential considerations should include understanding whether there are any company restrictions on the timing of the hedging trades. Also, a grantee must understand his attitude toward risk. Try to reduce risk, and avoid being a speculator. If you are an executive, will hedging of ESOs be viewed as an expression of negativism toward the company's future?

Preliminary Discussion

With all the proper due diligence and preparation outlined, we can now begin to think about what a hedging strategy would look like. So let's turn to some preliminary analysis. Unless specifically stated otherwise, the following discussion deals with nonqualified options. Of course, the assumption is that the restrictions against hedging are not prohibitive. The strategies explained here, furthermore, can be applied by executives (i.e., officers, directors, and holders of more than 10 percent of the company stock). However, executives must be concerned with Sections 16b and 16c of the Securities Exchange Act of 1934 and with SEC Rules 16b(3), 16c(4), and 10b(5).

Value Components of Options

Stock options consist of two distinct value elements. These valuation concepts are intrinsic value and time premium, which we explained in Chapter 3, but we will quickly review again here.

Intrinsic value equals the difference between the current market price of the stock and the exercise price of the options. When exercising and immediately selling the acquired stock, the grantee receives the intrinsic value minus the tax. Time premium equals the value of the options above the intrinsic value. Time premium, therefore, equals the nonintrinsic share of total value on an option, and is due to the probability that the stock will increase over time. Time premium is calculated by theoretical pricing models, and is a function of time to expiration and levels of implied volatility. All time premium is forfeited when ESOs are exercised prematurely, an approach promoted by most investment and financial advisers for reasons we mentioned previously.

Aim of the Hedging Strategy

Our objective is to indirectly capture 100 percent (or more) of the time premium and intrinsic value by systematically "writing" listed long-term calls or buying selected long-term puts. Of course, holding the employee options unhedged to expiration day can "capture" intrinsic value, but our strategy also reduces much of the risks of holding the options to expiration day. We believe it can capture more than 100 percent of the time premium. We also believe hedging reduces taxes to as low as possible. We accomplish these objectives by avoiding premature exercises. A premature exercise causes a forfeiture of the time premium and an early and sometimes unnecessary tax liability. As will be seen below, we emphasize that one principle over all others.

Fast Fact

By avoiding premature exercise through hedging, it is possible to achieve between a 40 percent and 100 percent average after-tax expected gain over what could be achieved by any conventional early exercise exit strategies.

Delta and Theta Risk Reduction

When options are granted, the initial position has what are called long deltas (i.e., bullish as an equivalent stock position) with negative thetas (i.e., erosion of the time premium). This means that ESOs lose value if the stock goes down, stays the same, or appreciates slightly. Time value is simply a function of passage of time and changes in implied volatility. We propose that, as an employee, you try to take an aggressive attitude toward reducing delta and theta risk. However, in the early days after the grant, we advise just minor risk reductions, given that on grant day none of the options are vested. We also do not want to interfere with the object of the options grant by substantially reducing the alignment of the interests of the employee with the interests of the employer early in the employment contract.

> **Long Delta**
>
> The risk and potential gain an ESO has when the stock price moves lower or higher, respectively. If there are 50 long deltas, this means, for example, that if the stock price decreases from $20 to $19, the ESO will lose about half the value that the stock positions gave up. However, delta is not fixed and will change as the stock moves lower or higher.

Applying the 7 Percent Solution

Immediately after being granted the ESOs, the first step in developing a hedge for ESOs involves selling (i.e., writing) listed calls equal to 7 percent of the number of options that have been granted. If substantial stock of the employer is held, a grantee should sell additional listed call options equal to 7 to 10 percent of the stock held.

At this point, total positions are very bullish and highly speculative (delta long), but less so than before the position became partially hedged with the sale of the calls. Risks have been reduced by approximately 5 to 7 percent compared to the time before you sold the listed calls. Upside potential profit has been reduced accordingly. We advise selling the longest listed long-term equity anticipation securities (LEAPS) calls, furthermore, which have exercise prices greater than or equal to the exercise prices of the granted employee options. However, the employee may want to sell different exercise prices, depending on how much the hedger wishes to reduce or maintain the delta and time value erosion risks.

Year-Two Adjustments

In year two following the options grant, sell the same number of listed LEAPS calls as in the first year, while maintaining the previously established short call positions. Again, after the sales of additional listed calls, risks and potential gain have been reduced accordingly. Perhaps a grantee has become vested in at least 20 percent of the options at this point, with about 7 percent of the long delta now removed. This leaves plenty of upside potential while taking out some of the downside risk.

Example

Let's assume that an employee has just received ESOs giving him the right to buy 10,000 shares of XYZ stock in a ten-year period to expiration. Leaving the issue of pricing aside for the moment, suppose he sells exchange traded calls equal to 7 percent of the ESOs (making the employee liable to deliver 700 shares of stock). We will further assume that he sells at-the-money LEAPS, so the delta on each is .60 for a total delta of −420 (the equivalent of being short 420 shares of stock. If he was long 10,000 in the form of ESOs, he would now be long just 9,580, although if the stock moves higher, the negative delta will approach −700 (maximum) and the net long delta would diminish accordingly. When he sells another 7 percent each year, he will be shaving off 420 deltas (assuming the price is fixed at the point you began selling calls), further reducing downside risk and upside potential, while leaving in place plenty of longside potential.

Adding More Short Deltas in Year Three

In year three, he would again consider repeating the selling of 7 percent more calls as earlier, depending on his attitude toward risk and where the stock is trading relative to the exercise prices. It would probably be good to keep the subjective choices to a minimum and stay with a consistent yearly objective, unless personal finance circumstances change.

Liquidation of Some Calls in Year Four

In the next year, he should repeat the selling of 7 percent more calls, consistent with the preceding steps. By this point, some of the option positions are probably showing a substantial gain and some are showing a loss. It would be wise to liquidate some of the losses and sell longer-term LEAPS calls as part of the strategy of reducing risk and taxes. Some of the options may have expired out-of-the-money. These could have created short-term capital gains or ordinary gains for the seller. Some of the options may have been exercised and the exercise notices assigned to the seller, making him short the stock. He could eliminate the short position in one of three ways: (1) deliver stock already owned outright, (2) buy stock to cover the short position and sell appropriate LEAPS calls, or (3) exercise ESOs and deliver the stock to cover the short stock. The third choice is the least attractive choice because it forfeits time premium and causes early tax consequences.

Repeating Year Four in Year Five

In the next year, repeat the selling of the calls as in the preceding steps, being conscious of the delta risks and the erosion risk and the possible tax consequences. Perhaps the employee is fully vested by now.

The Next Step

In the next years, do the same as in year five until the short calls are equal to 60 to 70 percent of all vested options. Executives must be careful of SEC Rule 16c(4), since most experts claim that an executive can sell calls only to the extent of his stock holdings. Our view is that an executive can sell out-of-the-money or at-the-money calls for each substantially in-the-money ESO long. Short calls should equal 60 to 100 percent of all stock owned. As time passes, the employee should roll back his short calls. This means that as the now "near-term" short calls approach expiration and have very little or no time premium remaining, buy them back and sell longer-term LEAPS, collecting thus more time premium.

There is a larger incentive to roll back the listed calls when there is a substantial short-term capital loss or ordinary loss to be taken.

In-the-Money ESOs

All in-the-money ESOs must be exercised prior to expiration day. Liquidate the proper number of shorted listed calls and liquidate stock received on exercise of the ESOs in a manner that minimizes risk and taxes, while maximizing capital gains. In the case where incentive stock options (ISOs) are held, large tax advantages can be achieved by holding the

EXHIBIT 13.1   Example of Total Call Positions throughout the Life of ESOs
Grant Day: calls short = 7% of ESOs and 7% of long stock
Grant day + 1yr : calls short = 14% of ESOs and 14% of long stk.
Grant day + 2 yr: calls short = 21% of ESOs and 21% of long stk.
Grant day + 3 yr: calls short = 28% of ESOs and 28% of long stk.
Grant day + 4 yr: calls short = 35% of ESOs and 35% of long stk.
Grant day + 5 yr: calls short = 42% of ESOs and 42% of long stk.
Grant day + 6 yr; calls short = 49% of ESOs and 49% of long stk.
Grant day + 7 yr: calls short = 56% of ESOs and 56% of long stk.
Grant day + 8 yr: calls short = 63% of ESOs and 63% of long stk.
Grant day + 9 yr: calls short = 70% of ESOs and 70% of long stk.

stock received upon exercise for over one year from the exercise date. In the case where ISOs are held, one may consider selling more than 7 percent (perhaps 8 to 10 percent) annually of the ISOs held. If an employee manages the ESOs properly, he can, in fact, increase his after-tax yield by over 50 percent on average relative to the "premature" exercise strategies. If the employee views the prospects of the employer more positively, then he should just strategically sell fewer calls during his time of bullishness.

If the employee's view of the company's prospects is less positive, then selling more LEAPS earlier is suggested. Perhaps he may sell as much as 15 percent per year, instead of 7 percent, until the total reaches 65 to 70 percent. The hedger may wish to time his call sales to be done, when officers and directors are exercising their ESOs and/or selling stock. The strategy outlined above accomplishes several objectives:

- Reduces risks (delta and theta and vega)
- Captures the time premium
- Reduces or eliminates taxes
- Preserves a limited bullish position during the life of the options, thereby keeping the employee's interests aligned with the interests of the company

This strategy recognizes that there is a high risk of getting zero from the grantee's employee stock options (see Chapter 4). The 7 percent solution assures that the grantee/employee will get something at least. In the case of insiders (i.e., officers, directors, and owners of 10 percent or greater of the company stock), special consideration must be made to comply with SEC rules and company restrictions. In certain circumstances, some parts of the 7 percent solution may not be available to such officers. Carrying out these strategies without training and assistance by experts requires a person to study this book and execute trades efficiently.

Example
MasterCard
Assumptions for a MasterCard Executive, April 6, 2009
Stock equals $171; options are granted to executive to purchase 10,000 shares at $171; options have contractual expiration date of 10 years from grant date; 20 percent of the options vest per year; early termination after vesting allows exercise within 90 days from termination; executive expects to be at the company until he retires in ten years; executive owns 10,000 shares of stock outright and expects to receive more options grants in the future; there are some restrictions on hedging; the executive has capital losses that he liquidated one year ago equaling $350,000; and he desires to reduce risks and taxes.

Recommended Trades
Immediately upon grant, the employee should sell 15 listed January $175, 2011 LEAPS calls for a price of $43.73 each, collecting $65,500 in option premium.

One year from grant, he should again sell 15 January $175, 2012 LEAPS calls options for market prices. Prices cannot be determined until day of sale. Prices should be near their theoretical values.

Two years from grant, sell 15 January near the money, 2013 LEAPS calls. Forty percent of the employee options should be vested by now. If the calls that were previously sold have expired or strategically closed, then new calls should be sold to maintain the intended hedge.

Three years from grant, sell 15 January near the money, 2014 LEAPS calls, looking for opportunities to take tax losses on earlier LEAPS calls written.

Four years from grant sell 15 January, 2015 LEAPS calls, while looking for opportunities to take tax losses and roll near-term short positions in calls to longer expiration dates to avoid assignments. Use the same approach in the following years until 65 percent of the employee stock options and 65 percent of long stock are covered by sales of listed LEAPS calls.

In the ninth and tenth years, try to reduce positions unless there has been more employee options or more stock granted. Be sure to exercise all in-the-money ESOs. If more options or stock have been granted, just start the process over again. What we have done so far is to hold a bullish position in MasterCard stock and options and captured time premium and reduced risk.

We have reduced the erosion risks and delta risks of holding naked stock and options from the initial day of grant. We have captured a large portion of the time premium that is often forfeited upon premature exercises. We will have delayed and minimized the tax liability. The exact details of what specific LEAPS calls should be sold and when to buy them back to achieve maximum results cannot be determined on day of grant but must be delayed to the future.

Alternative Strategy
If hedging with listed options against ESOs when prohibited by contract:

- Simply sell listed calls on five to ten stocks that have high positive correlation to the employer's stock. This may take a bit more accounting, but it may be the only way to efficiently hedge the risks of holding the ESOs.
- Since there is no restriction on selling positively correlated stock short or options, there is no need to be concerned with SEC or company restrictions.
- The only real problem in this method is that the five to ten stocks may not have a high tracking to the employer stock.

Does Hedging ESOs Undermine Alignment of Interests?

Right off the bat, we will tell you that hedging ESOs does not undermine the alignment of interests. In fact, hedging reduces risk and allows the ESO holders to hold the interest alignment longer. The grantee who exercises options and sells his stock loses 100 percent of his company alignment through those options as the majority of all stock received from exercises of nonqualified options is immediately sold.

The grantee who hedges his positions maintains a substantial portion of his alignment, especially those who merely hedge part of their ESOs. Whenever we speak with a person who has experience with ESOs, we generally get the comment that hedging defeats the object of the options grant. The person claims that the purpose of granting ESOs is to align the interest of the company with the interests of the employees. The claim is that hedging the ESOs essentially reduces the equity position of the employee, which defeats the object of the grant, and it should be discouraged by the employer. That idea is just another myth that pervades the ESO industry. Let's look at the idea closely. We will do so by way of an example with a few scenarios.

Stock Plus Employee Stock Options

Many employees these days own stock to go along with their ESOs. Let's assume that an employee owns 4,000 shares of stock and ESOs to buy 10,000 shares with an expiration date of five years from today. The options are exercisable at $50, with the stock trading at $70. In trader's lingo, the two combined positions may have a delta of long 12,200 shares (i.e., +4,000 from the stock and +8,200 from the ESOs). So, here, the employee could be perceived as owning the stock equivalent of 12,200 shares. Let's look at this through a few different scenarios.

> If he were to sell the 4,000 shares (which is not discouraged by the company), he would reduce his deltas by 4,000 shares and thereby reduce his alignment by 4,000 shares.
>
> If he were to prematurely exercise ESOs to purchase 4,000 shares and sell the stock, his deltas would be reduced by perhaps 3,280. This, of course, is not discouraged by the company after vesting, even though it will have reduced the executive's alignment with the company by 3,280 stock equivalents.
>
> If he were to sell his 4,000 ESOs on some new transferable options plan, his deltas would be reduced by 3,280, thereby reducing his alignment accordingly.
>
> If he were to sell (write) listed LEAPS calls on 4,000 shares of stock with an exercise price of $75 against the 4,000 shares, this would reduce his deltas by perhaps 2,400. His alignment would be lessened by the 2,400 deltas.

So why would the company discourage the last scenario we mentioned and not discourage the first three? Actually, discouraging hedging reduces the perceived value of ESOs in the eyes of the employee. This perceived reduction of value requires a larger grant to employees to create the same incentive. If the hedging was not discouraged, the employees would perceive the ESOs to have more value, thereby requiring fewer total options granted and thus fewer accounting costs to the employer.

Benefits

Basically, if companies were to encourage a gradual hedging of the ESOs from the date of grant to expiration, this would create more value in the eyes of the employees and require fewer grants and fewer expenses against earnings. This would also provide the employee an efficient way to exit his ESO positions, reduce risks, and delay taxes.

It can be reasonably speculated that there are other factors that come into play to explain the encouragement of early sales of stock and prematurely exercising ESOs, while at the same time discouraging the hedging of ESOs with listed calls. It is not, however, to increase the alignment of the dual interests.

Those factors are: (1) the company gains a reduced liability from premature exercises due to time premium forfeited back to the company, (2) the company gets a tax deduction immediately upon premature exercise, and (3) the company gets an infusion of cash immediately. These factors are the real reasons that the companies encourage premature exercises. Selling of stock is encouraged less than premature exercises are encouraged.

Conclusion

Discouraging hedging with listed options is essentially encouraging premature exercises.

Why Do Companies Want You to Exercise Prematurely?

I n previous chapters, the case against premature exercise was presented from the point of view of the employee's self-interest. Unless absolutely necessary because of a high value placed on the need for cash, avoiding premature exercise—and its associated large tax bite and forfeited time premium (in effect lowering compensation but without a tax benefit)—should be the rule for holders of ESOs.

Fast Fact

Unless absolutely necessary because of a high value placed on the need for cash, avoiding premature exercise—and its associated large tax bite and forfeited time premium (in effect lowering compensation but without a tax benefit)—should be the rule for holders of ESOs.

Many executives and their advisers do not fully understand the nature of ESOs, but they do know that early exercises benefit the company.

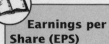

Earnings per Share (EPS)

The Financial Accounting Standards Board (FASB) requires companies' income statements to report Earnings Per Share (EPS) for each of the major categories of the income statement: continuing operations, discontinued operations, extraordinary items, and net income. The P/E ratio (price-to-earnings ratio) of a stock (also called its "P/E", or "earnings multiple") is a measure of the price paid for a share relative to the annual net income or profit earned by the firm per share. EPS equals Profit divided by the Weighted Average of Common Shares Outstanding.

This chapter is about why they want early exercises. In this chapter, therefore, the financial benefits to companies of premature exercise are explained, as well as exactly why companies prefer premature exercises.

Reasons Why Companies Like You to Exercise

Company executives are well aware of the fact that granted options prior to exercise represent potential dilution of their stock. This is because, upon exercise, the company typically issues new stock. So unless they buy stock in the marketplace, which often causes a strain on their cash, the earnings are diluted as measured by the well-known earnings-per-share ratio. Buying outstanding shares to meet exercises raises the earnings-per-share number.

But a company must report earnings fully diluted for outstanding options, whether the ESOs are exercised or not. So, from the standpoint of dilution of shares, whether the options are exercised makes little difference. What is more important, however, is that a part of the value of the options is forfeited by the grantee back to the company upon exercise. That part is the time premium, and it can be large or small, depending on the time remaining on the option and levels of volatility. Therefore, the premature exercise actually reduces the liability that the company has toward the grantee. The size of that reduction depends on the time premium forfeited and the volatility of the stock and the price of the stock vis-à-vis the exercise price.

FAST FACT

Part of the value of options forfeited by a grantee back to the company upon premature exercise reduces the liability that the company has toward the grantee. The size of that reduction depends on the time premium forfeited and the volatility of the stock and the price of the stock vis-à-vis the exercise price. But, overall, it is usually in the company's best interest.

When ESOs are exercised prematurely, there is a premature tax liability to the grantee and a premature compensation expense deduction for the company. This often results in a large positive cash flow for the company. There is also an infusion of cash, equal to the exercise price received by the company, unless the shares are purchased in the market to prevent dilution. Also, the precedent of a pattern of early exercises allows the company to use a lower assumed expected time remaining on the prospectively granted ESOs, thereby allowing a lower generally accepted accounting principles (GAAP) earnings expense.

Therefore, sufficient financial incentives exist for companies to encourage early exercises, which are by no means incidental. In addition, it must be understood that premature exercises are almost always followed by immediate sale of the stock. The result is that any alignment with the company that those unexercised ESOs presented is eliminated 100 percent.

GAAP Earnings

The most reliable earnings are so-called GAAP earnings, which are arrived at by using the Generally Accepted Accounting Principles. The Financial Accounting Standards Board, a nonprofit organization responsible for establishing principles of financial accounting and reporting, designs these rules.

Did You Know?

Companies encourage early exercises because they benefit from the early tax deductions and early infusion of cash.

The encouragement of premature exercises works to defeat the purpose of the options grant, yet often the same defenders of early exercise will make the argument that hedging severs the alignment of interests, despite the fact that few hedgers would encourage removing all upside potential of holding ESOs. In other words, hedging itself does not eliminate the alignment established by an option grant, but premature exercise and sale does break the so-called link established by the grant.

Chapter

ESO Hedging Case Studies

Google

In Chapter 13, we saw how a hedging plan (the "7 percent solution") would work. In this chapter, we take it one step further by looking at some case studies of hedging approaches applied to leading technology stocks. We will make some assumptions about the stock price, the value of the ESOs, and listed options and then examine how hedging would have helped maximize the value and minimize risk. We begin in this chapter with a look at hedging ideas for some Google ESOs, to be followed by additional case studies of Yahoo! and Apple ESOs that were hedged with listed options.

Analysis of a Hedge against Google ESOs

Let's assume that an employee has been granted ESOs by Google. Additionally, we will make the following assumptions to illustrate some hedging scenarios:

- We assume that Google common stock was trading for $200 per share and paying no dividend on February 7, 2005.
- We assume that on February 7, 2005, the employee was granted qualified options to purchase 1,000 shares at $200 per share.

- We assume that the options had ten years maximum contractual time to expiration when granted and that the options vest 33 percent per year.

- We assume that early termination will cause the expiration date to change from February 7, 2015, to 90 days after termination.

- We assume the correct volatility is .34 during a six-year option term.

- We assume a 4 percent interest rate for a six-year government bond as of February 7, 2005.

- We assume that the ESOs holder was confident that he would not be terminated or he will not terminate his employment within a six-year period after the grant.

- We assume that the grant of the options is exempt from Securities and Exchange Commission (SEC) Rule 16b, even though this may or may not be the case in all situations.

Theoretical Values of Google Calls

The theoretical value of Google's granted ESOs, given the assumptions spelled out earlier (i.e., the right to purchase 1,000 shares of Google stock at $200), would range from $86,000 to $89,000, and would represent time premium only.

There is no intrinsic value since the options are granted with a strike price equal to the stock price. The theoretical value of the two-year listed long-term equity anticipation securities (LEAPS) calls, with an exercise price of $200, would be approximately $4,800 per 100 shares using a .39 implied volatility assumption. Since these are at-the-money, they also represent pure time premium. The two-year LEAPS call options were selling for $4,800 (a price of $48 in premium multiplied by $100) on February 7, 2005.

We then make the assumption that four LEAPS were sold (written) and the proceeds totaled $19,200 (4 × $4,800 = $19,200). The employee/seller is obligated to deliver 400 shares to a holder of four LEAPS for $200 per share if and when the call holder exercises his option. Essentially, therefore, 40 percent of the 1,000 ISOs are hedged after the sale of the four LEAPS calls because of the short deltas of the four calls.

In the writer's view, the IRS Section 1092 and Section 1221 would not apply.

The total position is long about 554 deltas. But the deltas of the extra ESOs to purchase 600 shares are about +.79 each. The delta of the four call "time spreads" (i.e., long the 400 ESOs versus short listed LEAPs to purchase 400 shares) are about equal to 80 positive deltas in total.

Example
Delta Calculation

ESO deltas (600 shares) = +474 (these are at-the-money with a .79 delta)

LEAPS deltas (400 shares) = −236 (these are at-the-money with a .59 delta)

ESO deltas (400 shares) = +316 (these are at-the-money with a .79 delta)

Total deltas for the combined positions are +554.

Assume the stock is unchanged two years from the sale of the four LEAPS calls. The two-year LEAPS would be worthless (all time premium has gone to zero) and the employee would have made a short-term capital gain of $19,200 on the four LEAPS. However, the ten ESOs will have lost some theoretical value, but since they are longer-term options, they lose much less time premium than the LEAPS. How much less? Our estimate is that the ten ESOs would have decreased by $8 each, or a total loss of approximately $8,000. This leaves a net gain of $11,200 before taxes on the ESO hedge. Since these ESOs were qualified, the sale of the calls would not be eligible to be included in the definition of "hedging transaction" under IRS Section 1221. Therefore the gain would be short term capital gain. If the grantee had other capital losses, he could use those other losses to reduce the capital gains tax on the $19,200.

Assume a 25 Percent Rise in Google

Let's take a look at another scenario. What if the stock advanced $50 after the first two years following the establishment of the hedge outlined above? What, then, would the outcome be for the hedged ESO options after two years? The two-year LEAPS would have a value equal to $5,000 each since they were now expiring in the money by $50 ($250 stock price − $200 strike price = $50 in-the-money × 100 multiplier = $5,000).

The expiration in-the-money, however, caused only a loss of $2 per option (or $200). Recall that the options were sold for $48 each. Therefore, the premium received for selling them was $4,800 and the loss on each was $200, leaving an overall loss of just $800 ($200 × 4 = $800).

Meanwhile, we would expect the ESOs to each have increased by about $31 in theoretical value for a total pretax gain of $31,000. The net theoretical gain, therefore, would be about $30,200 with no taxes due at this time on the increased value of the ESOs. The loss on the LEAPS, meanwhile, represents a short-term capital loss and could be used as a deduction currently against other capital gains or $3000 yearly ordinary income.

Stock Decrease Scenario

A more interesting scenario develops if we assume the stock decreases. Here, we will project a fall in price of Google to $170 at expiration of the two-year life of the LEAPS. As in the first case above, the LEAPS would expire worthless and there would be a pretax gain of $19,200 on the LEAPS sold. There would be a theoretical loss on the ESOs approximately equal to $25 per ESO, or $25,000 total on the ESOs if we keep our assumptions of volatility and interest rates the same. There would then be a net theoretical loss of $5,800 ($19,200 − $25,000 = − $5,800) when the LEAPS and ESOs gains and losses are netted.

Of course, if the stock were substantially lower after the two-year period, the gain on the written LEAPS would have covered less of the theoretical loss on the ESOs.

The employee always has the opportunity to write additional listed LEAPS calls during the life of his ESOs, since he owns ISOs with a potential life of ten years, much longer than the two-year LEAPS holding period. Whatever happens in the interim in terms of the price of Google, the hedged ESOs will provide a safer return and, in the majority of cases, a greater return. Of course, a substantial portion of the potential gain is sacrificed when the sale of the four calls is made.

Updates

August 4, 2005, Google Update   Let's look at what actually transpired. On August 4, 2005, Google had increased to $297 from $200 when the hedge was put on. The four LEAPS calls that we sold on February 7,

2005 had increased from a market-traded value of $48 to $118.5. Even after a 97-point increase in the stock, there was still $20 of time premium on each of the four LEAPS call options, illustrating that the likelihood of a premature exercise of the LEAPS is still very small. Nobody would exercise a call option with that much time premium since they forfeit the value to the seller, meaning to the hedger in this case. It would be a good thing for the hedger if he received an assignment of the exercise notice.

The ISOs during this period of the price rise had increased in theoretical value from $88 to $170.5. The ten ISOs, therefore, had an increased theoretical value of $82,500 ($170.5 – $88 = $82.5 × 1,000 = $82,500). The theoretical value of the two positions when combined had increased by $54,300.

We would have advised closing out the four short LEAPS, paying $47,400, and immediately selling 6 January 2008 LEAPS calls with an exercise price of $290, for $48,300 in time premium collected (i.e., $8,050 × 6 = $48,300). The hedger is still able to report a short-term capital loss of $28,200 for tax purposes, unless the straddle rule applied, which we feel would not apply. The theoretical gain on the ISOs is not a gain for current tax purposes, and does not offset the $28,200 loss for tax purposes. The simultaneous purchase of the 4 calls together with the sales of the 6 January 2008 calls with an exercise price of $290 does not constitute a Wash Sale.

Did You Know?

Generally, when listed calls experience losses, the losses are short-term capital losses that can be used to offset capital gains you may have from other assets. We believe that when hedging ISOs, neither IRS Section 1221 nor 1092 apply. However, when nonqualified ESOs are hedged, IRS Section 1221 applies and considers the hedges to be "hedging transactions." This makes any gains and losses from the sale of the listed calls ordinary gains and losses.

Where does the employee stand at this point? His combined position is still bullish, and his equity has increased $54,300. Meanwhile, he has a tax deduction. Not too bad so far. Of course, had he not sold the four LEAPS calls, the theoretical equity would have increased by $82,500. But the point is to provide some downside risk and risk from time premium decay in exchange for giving up some upside potential. It is important to understand that hedging to reduce risk will sacrifice some—and in this case a substantial part—of the potential gains. The position can now be described as long a 6 × 6 call diagonal time spread (to use trading floor lingo) with four extra ESOs long.

The ISOs have an exercise price of $200 and the new 6 January 2008 calls that were sold have an exercise price of $290. The position is still net long delta and there is positive theta.

October 31, 2005 Google Update Google was trading at $368.75 (i.e., $71.75 higher than when the 6 January $290 calls were sold in 2008). The sale was at $80.50. The calls are now trading at $135.90 (i.e., $55.40 higher than the sale at $80.50 on August 4, 2005. The ISOs had increased in theoretical value from about $170.5 to $237 (i.e., $66.5 higher than their value on August 4, 2005).

> **Net Positive Theta**
>
> When an options strategist is net positive theta, this means that the position will gain from declines in time premium of the options, other things being equal. When an optionee sells calls against his or her ESOs, the total position will be net positive theta if the negative theta on the ESOs is smaller than the positive theta on the listed LEAPS call options that he or she sold.

The implied volatilities in the Google options have increased and the interest rates have increased, thereby adding value to both the listed calls and the theoretical value of the ISOs.

We have seen again a net increase in value of $11,100 ($66,500 − $55,400 = $11,100), with the $71.75 increase in Google stock.

In other words, if the hedger had been able to buy back the 6 listed LEAPS calls and "roll" the sale to a different LEAPS call strike, he would be able to report an additional short-term capital loss of $32,400 with no taxable gain on the ISOs (i.e., if the straddle rule would not have applied). If nothing was done, then the deltas would be still be somewhat long.

June 7, 2006, Google Update Google stock was trading at $386.51 on June 7, 2006. The January 2008 calls with a $290 strike price were selling for $143.30. With the stock $89 higher from the time we sold the January 2008 calls with a strike price of $290, the calls were $63 higher. The price of $143.30 indicated an implied volatility of .42. This indicated an implied volatility for the ISOs of .39. Therefore, the theoretical value of the ISOs would be $248.

The theoretical value of the ISOs, therefore, increased more than the market value of the $290 calls since August 5, 2005, partly because volatilities and interest rates increased accordingly. The employee could have closed the six written calls of January 2008 with a strike price of $290 and sold 8 January 2008 calls with a strike price of $390. The market value of the $390 calls was $82.5 per call. The closing purchase of the 6 January 2008 $290 calls resulted in a $37,800 short-term capital loss. The ISOs have increased $82,000 in theoretical value since August 5, 2005, which is not currently taxable. So we had another net increase with capital tax deductions. Eventually, the optionee will have to pay a tax on the ISOs, but there is much that can be done over the next six to eight years to solve that possible issue.

July 29, 2006, Google Update   Since June 7, 2006, Goggle stock had gone up $2 at $388.50. But the January 2008 $390 calls have decreased $5.5, giving an unliquidated profit of $4,400. The ISOs would have been unchanged in our theoretical estimation. We would not buy in the written calls, especially if the hedger is an executive subject to the Section 16b of the Securities and Exchange Act of 1934.

> **Net Long Delta**
>
> When an options strategist is net long delta, this means that the position will gain from rise in the stock price and lose from a decline in price, other things held equal. When an optionee sells calls against his or her ESOs, the position will be net long if the negative delta on the short calls is smaller than the positive delta of the ESOs.

If an employee were subject to Section 16b, considering all factors, he would probably just hold the position. Google

> **Tip**
>
> Section 16b of the Securities and Exchange Act of 1934 makes any profits earned by officers and directors when selling or buying equity securities of their company within 6 months of each other recoverable by the company. Grants of equity compensation are considered a buy when the grant occurs. However, the SEC has promulgated rules that generally exempt the grants from being included under Section 16b.
>
> Writing calls and buying them back within 6 months at a profit would be subject to Section 16b making the profit recoverable by the company.
>
> Buying stock and then selling the stock at a profit within a six month period makes the officer or director strictly liable to have the profits recovered by the company.

reported reasonably good earnings, and there was little to make the stock volatile in the short run.

August 14, 2006, Google Update: Adding a Long Straddle   If the employee were a noninsider, and he had sold 8 January $390 calls written against the ten ISOs with $200 strike (mentioned above), he could buy four January 2008 $410 calls and four January 2008 $380 puts. The straddle would go for about $107.4, which could be easily accomplished with a limit order. If he put on this position, there would have been a reasonable chance of an extreme move in either direction, a move that is greater than the volatility the market value of the options implied.

The preceding positions (i.e., long ISOs and short calls and/or long puts) would have resulted in total gains with the stock rising. However, the gain would be less than the gain would have been had no hedging been done. With the stock below the exercise price of the LEAPS, or just a small amount above the exercise price, the hedged positions would have done much better than just holding "naked" ISOs.

As of the writing of this chapter in 2009, Google was below 480. Continuing with the same strategy, the employee would have achieved in our view, overall gains with current tax deductions.

Yahoo!

In the previous case study, we saw how hedging Google ISOs produced a less risky after-tax net gain than simply holding ISOs unhedged. In this chapter, we look at Yahoo! ESOs and how hedging might have improved the outcomes.

Analysis of Hedging Yahoo! ESOs

Let's assume that on May 1, 2003, an executive was granted options giving him the right to purchase 20,000 shares of Yahoo! at $25, and that these options had maximum expiration date ten years from the day of the grant. The stock would later trade at $32, with expected time to expiration of five years. Suppose, furthermore, that the executive was granted 10,000 shares of restricted stock that had vested and the taxes were fully paid. He became worried that the market was heading south, and wants to reduce his total risk.

Now let's assume that there have been no additional grants for the past six months, and he does not expect another for nine months. Here is what he could have done to hedge using listed options. If he wanted to reduce 50 to 65 percent of the risk, he could have sold 300 listed LEAPS calls on the company stock with an exercise price of $35. One hundred of the calls would be considered "qualified covered calls" covered by the 10,000 shares, and 200 would be considered "naked" by his broker, normally requiring margin.

But if he deposits the fully paid-for shares of stock, the margin requirement is eliminated on the covered and "naked" writes, even when no consideration is given to the fact that he holds the 20,000 ESOs. Most brokerage firms require excessive margin for writing "naked" calls. But there are some very good brokers who do not charge excessive margin.

Tip
Research margin costs. Visit www.cboe.com/micro/margin/strategy.aspx for an explanation of margin rules.

Let's look at market prices of the January 2008 LEAPS calls, which had an implied volatility of .31. On May 1, 2006, with Yahoo! at $32, the January 2008 calls, having a strike price of $35, were selling for $5.15 each. If he sold 300 of these calls at $5.15, he would receive $154,500 ($5.15 × 300 × 100 multiplier = $154,500), which would be credited to an options trading account immediately. The executive can take most of the $154,500 out to spend or reduce his credit card balances or buy certificates of deposit.

He can take the money out, without tax or borrowing. No interest charges will be applied, and if he has a good broker, he might even be allowed to earn interest on the money while it sits in the account. If the broker will not allow what we are suggesting, he should find another broker.

Stock Equivalent Position

Stock equivalent position is the total of stock position added to the summed deltas of options to get a total that is roughly equivalent to holding a certain amount of stock.

Before the sale of the 300 LEAPS calls, the total deltas (or stock equivalent position) was long 27,000 shares. This number is calculated by taking 10,000 granted shares and combining with 20,000 ESOs having a delta of .85 each. The stock equivalent position prior to selling the listed calls, therefore, is the 17,000 ESOs (20,000 × .85 = 17,000) plus 10,000 shares of granted stock, or 27,000 shares. After the sales of the LEAPS calls with a strike price of $35, the total deltas became a 10,000 long deltas stock equivalent position. The call deltas total –17,100 equivalent short stock. When we subtract this from the 27,000 long deltas, we are left with 10,000 positive deltas (27,000 long – [30,000 × .57 deltas] = positive 10,000 deltas) (see Exhibit 16.1).

At this point, he would have reduced his risk by 61 percent and still maintains a net long delta position. He would have received the proceeds of the 300 LEAPS calls immediately. Essentially, he sold some of his employee stock options at market prices. He owes no tax and forfeited no time premium back to the company. The above scenario was modeled on Yahoo!. Under the preceding scenario, the grantee is still long the equivalent of 10,000 shares of stock immediately after the write of the listed calls. The net value of the sum of all positions will have increased if the stock advanced. There is the possibility of a margin call if the stock moved substantially higher in the short run, yet this is remote. He could have decreased the risk of a margin call by selling fewer LEAPS calls, perhaps 250 instead of 300. However, he would have less protection on the downside.

If the stock goes to $43 and there is a margin call, there is nothing to worry about. All he has to do is make an adjustment in his account. For example, he could cover 100 of the $35 calls, sell 70 of the $45 calls, and sell 1,500 shares of the stock. Alternatively, he could also return some of the $154,000 from call premium collected, or exercise a very small number of the ESOs and deposit that stock into the trading account. Executives have to be careful of buys and sells within six months of grant day.

EXHIBIT 16.1 Prehedge Stock Equivalents versus Posthedge Stock Equivalents			
Prehedge		*Posthedge*	
10,000 shares	= +10,000	10,000 shares	= +10,000
20,000 ESOs	= +17,000	20,000 ESOs	= +17,000
		Short 300 listed calls	= –17,000
Total	= +27,000	Total	= +10,000

Taxes from the Yahoo! Hedge

It is our view that the gains or losses on the sale of the options would have been treated for tax purposes the following way: The gain or loss on 100 covered calls should be treated as short-term capital gain or loss when liquidated because the sale of 100 of the calls would be considered "qualified covered calls" and are thus not subject to the IRS Straddle Rule Section 1092. The loss on the 200 naked calls would not be subject to the straddle rule but would be subject to IRS Section 1221. Therefore, any liquidated loss would be ordinary loss under IRS Section 1221.

Updates

July 19, 2006, Yahoo! Update On July 19, 2006, Yahoo! dropped over $6 to around $26. The January 2008 ($35) calls were trading at $2.30 to $2.35. What should the hedger have done at this time as the long deltas increased when the short calls lost negative deltas as they moved farther out-of-the-money? He could have sold part of the stock or sold more calls or done nothing. My advice would have been to sell a few more calls (25) with a strike price of $30 using the January 2009 LEAPS calls, or sell some shares of stock (especially if some of the Yahoo! stock would give a capital tax loss). Either choice would reduce the long deltas of the summed positions. If he were an officer or director, he would not want to buy the written calls back under any circumstances or, for that matter, any other calls or stock. Section 16b of the Securities Act of 1934 would require that the gains are returnable to the company if they are made within 6 months. An executive must wait until six months after he made the trade to record a gain.

November 8, 2006, Yahoo! Update On November 8, 2006, Yahoo! stock was trading at $27 with the January 2008 $35 calls trading at $1.70 to $1.80. Writers of the January 2008 $35 calls would have an unliquidated profit of $3.35 on each call sold. Buying those calls back would cause a taxable event, which should be avoided or delayed unless there are liquidated or unliquidated capital losses to offset those gains.

Buying back 100 of those January 2008 $35-covered calls at $1.75 and selling 60 of the January 2009 $30 calls at $5.30 will reduce the delta and gamma risk and still preserve the positive erosion of the hedge. The executive would have also received another check without tax or borrowing. Of course, the closing of the sale of the 100 calls creates a short-term capital gain.

Apple Computer, Inc.

In the previous two sections, ESOs that an employee held in Yahoo! and Google were hedged under different assumptions, but using actual market and theoretical prices for the stock, ESOs, and the listed options. Here, we will continue with case studies analysis, using an example based on Apple Computer, Inc.

> **Qualified Covered Calls**
>
> A "qualified covered call" must meet three basic requirements: (1) the call cannot be too much in-the-money, (2) the calls must be listed on an options exchange, and (3) the calls must have at least 30 days remaining to expiration but not more than 33 months when sold (written). If the option had more than 12 months to expiration, the strike price would have to be adjusted to comply with the "qualified covered call status" of recent Treasury Regulations.

Analysis of Hedging Apple Computer ESOs

Let's assume that an employee had been granted 5,000 shares of Apple restricted stock six years ago. Furthermore, suppose this restricted stock position vested five years ago when the stock was $30 and that he had paid the tax on the stock, and that he has not liquidated the position yet. Additionally, let's assume he was granted 10,000 ESOs 4.5 years ago with an exercise price of $27 and that these options are now vested. If he wants to efficiently reduce risk and incur profits without paying a large tax bill, here is how.

Apple on April 26, 2007

Apple had a market price at the close on April 26, 2007, of $98.84. To do a viable hedge with upside profit potential, he would sell (write) 150 January 2009 LEAPS calls with an exercise price of $110. These are about 10 percent out-of-the-money. The sale could have been made at a price of $16.20 for each call option. The sale of the 50 January 2009 calls would not create a straddle under Section 1092 nor a "hedging transaction" under IRS Section 1221 because the 50 calls are considered "qualified covered calls." The sale of the other 100 calls will, in our view, be considered a "hedging transaction" under IRS Section 1221.

Proceeds in the amount of $243,000 from the calls sold would be credited to his account. At some firms that charge the minimum margin requirements, the writer could remove all of the proceeds of the sale of the calls and still have substantial excess margin. There would be no borrowing or interest. In fact, with the new portfolio minimum margin requirements, the writer of the 150 calls would be required to own only 2,000 shares fully paid for in order to satisfy initial margin requirements.

Tip

Customer portfolio margin (CPM) is now available at most brokerages. To qualify, the grantee would need to have at least $100,000 in equity in his account. The reduced margin with these newer margin rules (in effect since April 2006) dramatically changes the margin requirement of hedging, which is demonstrated in this chapter. To read more about CPM, visit the margin pages at the Chicago Board Options Exchange (CBOE) and the Options Clearing Corporation (OCC) web sites.

No taxes or interest payments would be accessed upon the withdrawal of the $243,000. The equivalent stock position prior to the sale (write) of the 150 calls was long 14,700 (i.e., 5,000 shares + 9,700 long deltas from your now deep-in-the-money ESOs). The equivalent stock position after the write would be reduced by 8,550 negative deltas (150 × .57 deltas × 100 = 8,550 negative deltas), making the new position that is net positive 6,150 deltas (i.e., net long the underlying stock).

There would have been no time premium forfeited back to the company. There would have been no current tax liability. There is no additional margin required to initiate this position. The deltas are still long 6,150. The delta risk has been reduced 60 percent. Erosion risk has been reduced by 100 percent. There is no longer the risk of negative theta (meaning the grantee is not losing any money from time premium decay).

If Apple goes down at this point, or stays the same or increases slightly, there will be a profit on the written calls over time. If the written calls are bought back at a profit or they expire worthless, a tax liability is created. The profit would probably be a short-term capital gain for the 50 "qualified covered calls," which could be offset by any unused past or prospective liquidations where the employee incurred capital losses.

Margin Collateral

Margin Collateral is generally stock or other securities that can be deposited into a margin account to provide the margin that must be advanced to initiate and maintain certain positions with a broker. Margin collateral is often deposited in lieu of cash.

If the Apple stock rises substantially after the write, however, the written calls will experience a loss. But the gain on the stock and ESOs will be substantially more than the loss on the written Apple calls. The losses on the written calls will generate potential tax losses and can be taken now or used in future years. Of course, if the grantee has no Apple stock or assets other than the Apple ESOs, he may consider making some premature exercises and sales of the stock to reduce delta risk and to provide any required margin for hedging. If the ESOs are qualified ESOs, the stock should be held and used as margin collateral.

Efficient hedging by selling Apple listed long-term out-of-the-money calls will result in 50 to 70 percent more earnings on average in any of the preceding circumstances with Apple than the naive strategy of premature exercises of options, sales of stock, and diversification.

Updates

May 14, 2007 Apple Update II: Stock Trading at $109.6   When Apple stock was trading about $109.6 on May 14, 2007, the January 2009 $110 calls were trading at $22.80. The value of the three positions combined increased about $60,000 with an unliquidated loss on the calls sold (written) of about $97,000.

So now the grantee could buy 50 of those short calls back and sell 50 of the January 2009 $120s, which would give him a liquidated $32,400 short-term capital loss and would make the position a bit more bullish (more long deltas). The spread (buying back the short January $110s and selling the January $120s) could be bought for about $430, or $21,500 (50 × $430 = $21,500). This would not be a Wash Sale in our view. Alternatively (or in addition to), he could buy 70 of the 150 January 2009 $110 calls back and sell 50 of the January 2009 $90s. Both of these are margin-reducing and capital loss–"harvesting" trades.

May 31, 2007, Apple Update III: Stock Trading for $120   Let's assume that the grantee took the earlier suggestion to buy 50 call verticals (bought 50 January $110 calls that he was already short and sold 50 of the $120 calls) for $430 each and/or bought another 70 January 2009 $110 calls against the sale of the 50 January 2009 $90 calls. At the higher stock price, Apple trading at $120, he can now buy back 30 January 2009 $110 calls and sell 30 January 2009 $130 calls, again "harvesting" capital losses and picking up some long deltas. That is what the grantee could have done and would be a typical recommendation, from our point of view.

June 7, 2007, Apple Update IV: Stock Trading for $123.65   With Apple's stock at $123.65 on June 7, 2007, the January 2010 calls would be available now for trading. He could now buy 50 percent of his short calls written in the January 2009 series having a strike of $120, and then sell an equal number of January 2010 calls with a strike of $140. This would produce a credit of 50 cents per option, but a realized loss. Again we harvest capital losses and hold onto unliquidated gains. These trades also pick up some additional long deltas and reduce margin requirements. Meanwhile, the implied volatility increase that has occurred in the marketplace, and the increase in interest rates, has added theoretical value to the ESOs and the listed calls.

> **Implied Volatility Increase**
>
> When implied volatility increases in an option market, other things remaining the same, this reflects increases in time premium. If you are short options on balance, this generates a decrease in equity; if you are long options on balance, it generates an increase.

June 12, 2007, Apple Update V: Stock Trading at $117   At this point, the grantee could close out losing short call positions in January 2009 series for tax harvest purposes. He would do this for all of the calls except the January 2009 calls with a strike of $90. This means he would buy back the January 2009 calls having a strike price of $130, or those having a strike price of $120. Meanwhile, he would be selling simultaneously the January 2010 calls having a strike of $130 and strike of $120. These adjustments would be done using a limit order, which gives a slight theoretical edge. Executives, however, must avoid profitable buys and sales within any six-month period if subject to Section 16b of the Securities Exchange Act of 1934.

July 13, 2007 Apple Update VI: Stock Trading at $137.7   Here, the executive could buy back all the January 2009 calls with a strike of $130 and then sell all January 2010 calls with a strike price of $150. He would get a 30-cent credit but take a loss on the adjustment. This adjustment again harvests tax losses and adds a small amount of positive deltas.

Implied Volatility Increase

The implied volatilities on the Apple calls have increased, making it such that the profits on the three positions combined were less than expected if the volatilities had stayed the same. Since April 27, 2007, when this Apple analysis started, there has been a general rise in the implied volatility of many stocks. Apple's implied volatility has risen from perhaps .33 to .41. Given the preceding factors, the value of the Apple listed calls has risen in both theoretical and market values. If a person had sold calls as described in this article, reducing his deltas accordingly, but remaining substantially long, he would have still expected a large rise in total value of his combined positions with the stock rising as it did. However, the rise would have been substantially less due to the rise in the implied volatility, although the theoretical value of the ESOs would have risen somewhat as a result of the rise in volatility.

The lesson here is that as time passes, volatilities and interests rates do change, thereby affecting the value of both the ESOs and the listed calls. That is why the prudent approach is to do hedges early after the grant with relatively small sales of calls and increase positions as time passes.

Mismatched Tax Losses and Gains

Some pundits claim that there will be a mismatching of losses and gains, with the losses on the listed calls not deductible against the ordinary income from the ESOs. Our analysis tells us that there is little to worry about with the idea of mismatched losses and gains, as long as the summed positions are always substantially positive delta.

ESO Valuation Methods

Beginning in 2006, the Financial Accounting Standards Board (FASB) and the Securities and Exchange Commission (SEC) required companies to value ESOs on the day of grant and expense that value against company earnings as the options vest. In their ruling, the FASB and the SEC recommended ways to value the ESOs. One way was to use the classic Black-Scholes valuations model. Another way was to use the binomial model, an alternative to the Black-Scholes model.

Did You Know?

The **Binomial options valuation model** provides a generalizable numerical method for the valuation of options given a price change in the option's underlying instrument. This price change is modeled via the **Binomial pricing model**, which is a discrete-time model of the varying price over time of financial instruments. The model allows for points of time within the valuation date and the expiration date of an option to be specified as a result of the method used by the pricing model.

Use of either model allowed using "expected" times to expiration rather than the maximum contract time to expiration. This treatment grows out of the fact that there is an expectation that a grantee holding ESOs might exercise his options prematurely. Or he might terminate his employment with the company prior to the expiration date of the ESOs.

It was also indicated by the SEC/FASB that it was permitted to consider ESOs differently from exchanged-traded calls because ESOs are not transferable or pledgable and sometimes not hedgable. However, the amount that was allowed for the reduction in value of the ESOs was not specifically determined by the FASB or the SEC. The method of reducing the value of the ESOs was left up to the discretion of the company, as was the amount of such reductions. In our view, the allowed reductions of value of the ESOs at the grant date was and is overstated, causing an understatement of the true expense to the company, thus boosting the bottom line.

Valuation and Volatility Assumptions

Valuing ESOs and listed options also requires assigning a volatility to them. Again, there is some uncertainty associated with the choice of volatility to be assumed in the models. Companies generally choose a low-volatility assumption to keep a lid on the value of the expensed ESOs (recall that higher level of assumed volatility means a higher theoretical price of the ESOs). In some cases, for example, companies assumed expected times to expiration to be as little as 35 percent of the maximum time to expiration and made additional reductions in the value of the ESOs due to their nonliquidity. These same companies made assumptions about the future volatilities that were far below what was justified.

The result of these skewed assumptions was that the accounting costs of the ESO grants were very understated and their generally accepted accounting principles (GAAP) earnings were overstated. Of course, that scenario played well for executives who saw their stocks rise as their earnings were overinflated. This provided the opportunity for executives to make premature exercises of earlier granted ESOs with the immediate sale of stock. Although these executives forfeited the time premium and were required to pay an early tax on compensation, in many cases the compensation committees made disguised reloads of new options, which made up for the time premiums forfeited and the early tax liability.

Comparing Restricted Stock with ESOs

Some companies and their grantees are beginning to understand that holding ESOs over long periods is very speculative and fraught with high risk. Some believe that restricted stock may offer a better alternative. This chapter explains the attraction of restricted stock compared to ESOs.

Restricted Stock versus ESOs

There has been much discussion claiming the demise of ESOs, with restricted stock taking over as a result of the required expensing of ESO grants. Let's compare the two concepts:

- Restricted stock often has vesting periods similar to the vesting periods of employee stock options—perhaps one to five years. There is not much difference here.

- Restricted stock generally has no restrictions after the vesting period. The stock can be sold immediately. ESOs can never be sold and rarely transferred even after vesting. But ESOs can be exercised after vesting any time prior to expiration.

This difference in liquidity makes restricted stock more appealing to the employee and less appealing to the employer. Most restricted stock is sold immediately after the stock vests. The greater liquidity of restricted stock results in shorter periods of employee/employer interest alignment, which to some degree defeats the purpose of the equity grant. However, some companies require executives to hold much of their restricted stock even after vesting. That requirement seems to help the company and the employee.

Fast Fact

Most restricted stock is sold immediately after the stock vests.

Taxable Compensation Income

The intrinsic value of the ESOs when exercised. ESOs are taxable compensation income. It is as if you were paid an amount equal to the intrinsic value. There is income tax withholding and a charge for social security subtracted when exercised, whether the stock is sold or not.

Generally taxable compensation income is assessed to the employee when the restricted stock vests, whether the stock is sold or held. Because the vesting of restricted stock triggers an early tax liability, a sale of at least 40 percent of stock to pay the tax usually follows immediately.

However, the tax on employee options can be delayed until expiration day, perhaps ten years from the grant day. There is no income tax liability when the options vest. This factor makes stock options more attractive to the employee, although the employer would like early exercises.

The common stock is always more valuable than the ESOs to buy the common stock. The stock could be as much as two to five times as valuable as the ESOs on grant day, depending mainly on the assumed volatility of the stock and the expected time remaining to expiration. Therefore, employers will grant far fewer shares of restricted stock than ESOs to purchase the same number of shares, if the object is to make an equally valued grant.

In order for the employer to grant restricted stock equivalent to the fair or theoretical value of ESOs, a theoretical value calculation of the options is required. The employer then determines how many shares of restricted stock equals the theoretical value of the ESOs that would have otherwise been granted.

Granting Stock

Granting restricted stock is far simpler than granting ESOs. The value of the stock is certain for the employee and the employer (at least those that are traded daily). Simplicity helps both the employer and the employee.

There is never the concern for the proper management techniques of restricted stock as there is for ESOs.

Employees can manage the ESOs to get more value than what the employer anticipates to be the options' fair value. There is no such opportunity for the employee with restricted stock.

ESOs generally result in an alignment of the interests of the employer with the interests of the employee for a longer period of time, since restricted stock can be sold immediately after vesting. Early exercising of ESOs forfeit value back to the company and creates an early tax liability for the employee. This gives informed employees holding employee options an incentive to hold the options longer and stay at the company longer. ESOs, in this regard, work in the favor of both the employer and the employee.

The employer, when granting ESOs, is now faced with calculating the theoretical value of the options on grant day and expensing that value over the vesting period. This, of course, works as a negative for the employer that grants ESOs, if the employer reports GAAP earnings. This consideration of expensing "fair value" is what is encouraging employers to switch part of their equity compensation to restricted stock.

Conclusion

Restricted stock is certainly a more stable asset than ESOs. Option values change for so many reasons. The ESOs' time premium erodes over time. The theoretical values of the ESOs decrease as volatility goes down. ESOs decrease as interest rates decrease and as dividends increase. But when the stock flies on the upside, ESOs explode with a "bang, not a whimper."

Google Transferable Options

On December 12, 2006, Google announced a plan to create transferable stock options for employees other than officers and directors. Their new nonqualified ESOs and some existing nonqualified ESOs became transferable. The expressed idea was to give holders of Google ESOs some added liquidity and value. In a detailed news release, Google was asked: "Why did Google create this program?" Google replied by stating:

> We want to permit Google employees to capture the "time premium" of their options. Because the current option program does not allow the sale of employee stock options, employees are able to realize value from the options only by exercising and then selling the stock at a price higher than the exercise price. With this program, employees will be able to realize not only the intrinsic value (the difference between grant price and market price for Google stock), but also the time premium of their options. Financial institutions such as banks may be willing to pay a premium above the intrinsic value for many options because of the time premium.

Only time will tell if Google achieves its objectives. But as of July 2009 the plan is a bust. No other company has imitated the Google Plan.

Implications of Transferables

Although many details of the plan had not been announced at the time the above statement was made, one important point had been disclosed. When the ESOs with more than two years to expiration are sold, the expiration date for the new options owner will change to two years from the purchase date. This has important implications. In other words, if an employee owns stock options that are vested and have five expected years remaining to expiration, he can sell the options to the Morgan allied bidders, but he receives only two years' time premium minus the bidders' costs and profit, whatever that may be.

For example, assume an employee owns vested ESOs to buy 1,000 shares of Google at $300, with the stock trading at $460. The expected volatility is .29, and the expected expiration is five years from now. The fair value of the options is $240,000 (i.e., $160,000 of intrinsic value plus $80,000 of time premium). If he exercises and sells the received stock, he will make the intrinsic value minus tax, netting about $100,000. If he sells the options to the Morgan bidders, he will receive the fair value of only a two-year option minus the Morgan bidders' costs and profits (i.e., $195,000 – the bidders' costs and profits). The net would be about $116,000 after tax.

Closer Analysis

Since the Google ESOs could not be transferred prior to the new transferable plan, the employee above, like many other employees, probably would have, prior to the Google transferable ESOs, ended up making premature exercises to obtain some cash from their in-the-money options. This results in forfeiture of the remaining time premium back to the company. Very few employees exercise their options at the end of the expiration period, choosing instead an earlier date. The transferable options, it is thought, would allow any employee holding ESOs to cash in by selling the ESOs and thereby capturing any intrinsic value along with some of the remaining time premium. Sounds like it could be a good idea to me. But is it really?

The following paragraphs describe some of the criticisms:

The prices that are to be bid by the Morgan allied bidders will be below fair value for two-year options unless a large group of traders is allowed to participate as buyers. Google indicated that the Morgan bidders expect to buy the ESOs at the bid price and to then hedge by shorting the stock (or perhaps by writing other calls as most expert traders would do).

This writer and his associates personally did just that as members of the Chicago Board Options Exchange (CBOE) and the Pacific Stock Exchange (PSE) for ten years using strategies that we created in the late 1970s and early 1980s.

They Must Sell at a Discount

The Morgan allied buyers will want a discount to theoretical value because of three factors:

1. They must hold the options until expiration, making the options somewhat illiquid. However, if the bidders are allowed to hedge by selling listed long-term equity anticipation securities (LEAPS), the capital tied up by having to hold the stock options to expiration would be minimal.

2. There are many risks associated with buying long-term calls and shorting stock to hedge. For example, there is the erosion risk and changing volatility and interest rates risks. Hedging by writing listed long-term calls, if allowed by Google, may not be that easy, as the markets in long calls are sometimes quite wide, although lately the markets seem to be tighter.

3. The buyers will be buying options that will have unique exercise prices and unique times to expiration. Unless the bidders are highly competent, that may cause some calculation issues.

These three factors will require buyers to look for a bit more profit per trade, meaning lowering bids to the employees looking to sell their ESOs. As a grantee, however, rather than selling the ESOs to the Morgan allied bidders, the grantee could hedge with the same options that the Morgan bidders would use to hedge. If he owned Google stock, he could easily hedge with no margin and receive all of the proceeds of the sale of the call options. If he had no stock, however, he would have to advance some margin in the form of cash or securities. With the new margin rules promulgated in April 2006, however, this would be a small sum compared to old margin requirements.

Hedging Can Capture 100 Percent of Time Premium

If the Google grantee chose to hedge rather than sell to the Morgan bidders, he can capture 100 percent of the time premium instead of a portion, and he would be able to delay his tax liabilities. Contrary to what many pundits claim, there are no prohibitions on hedging Google stock other than during "lockout" periods, where grantees are required to refrain from buying or selling company securities. We have referenced the Google options plan and a Google options agreement, which "constitute the entire agreement of the parties"

A. An employee and holder of vested ESOs with expected five years to expiration could capture the time premium from the two-year options two and one half times by writing the calls. Margin requirements and the like are not prohibitory. Any Google employee should have enough assets to carry some margin positions. If the Google employee holds stock, there may be no additional margin requirement and the proceeds could be removed.

B. The transferable plan will encourage the ESO holders to sell their equity positions a bit earlier than otherwise, thereby reducing the mutual alignment of interests. However, sales of ESOs with more than two years remaining will still forfeit some time premium, depending on the time remaining on the ESOs greater than two years.

C. The plan may result in lower volatility of the stock, thereby diminishing the value of all outstanding Google ESOs and listed options. The reason why this will happen is beyond the scope of this book. On the day after the announcement, we saw drops in the market prices of all long term out-of-the-money and at-the-money listed options in Google. This actual value decrease may dissipate over time. But as traders know, the constant stream of options sale orders lowers implied volatility, which may last for long periods. The general implied volatility in Google has decreased from 30 to 27 shortly after Google's announcement in December.

D. The time premium that was forfeited to Google in the past by early exercises will now be divided up between Google, the Morgan bidders, and the employee, rather than 100 percent previously going to Google. This plan will raise the costs to Google because of two factors:

1. The fair value of the options at grant will be increased slightly (5 to 10 percent), thereby causing higher accounting expenses. Google says that the increased fair value of ESOs will cause a $260 million write-off on the existing 6.6 million ESOs that will become transferable. The idea that the transferable feature will add $39.39 of fair value to the average option is incorrect. This means that Google will write off an expense of $39.39 on 6.6 million outstanding options each. This, in my view, is far out of line, unless Google was far overstating the lack of transferability in its earlier calculations of fair value.

2. The forfeited time premiums, although less than in the past, will no longer all go to Google, thereby increasing real expenses. Google has indicated that they may reduce the number of options granted to offset the added costs.

E. Over time, Google will find its employees with fewer holdings of ESOs, thereby requiring a "reload" of options to maintain the same alignment of mutual interests.

> **Fair Value**
>
> Fair Value in the context of employee stock options is the value arrrived at by inputting various data, like volatility, expected time to expiration, interest rates, dividends and the relationship of the stock to the exercise price into a theoretical pricing model.

Conclusion

Unless we are missing something, it is a big loser for Google if they indeed have to write off $260 million to add the transferability feature. It is a big winner for Morgan and its bidders. It is positive for the employees who need to cash in early. To the average sophisticated grantees, the transferable feature has little value. If Google cuts back on the number of ESOs granted to employees to offset the transferability factor and alleged costs, the employees will have a net loss. Of course, the plan does represent an improvement for the employee over the strategy of premature exercise, followed by selling stock and diversifying. It also allows the sale of out-of-the-money ESOs after vesting, thereby receiving something for the out-of-the money options.

However, there is a much easier way to design a plan to accomplish Google's objectives with very little costs to Google and substantial benefits to Google's employees. If Google wants the employees to "capture time premium," all they have to do is reload the grantee with new ten-year options whose fair value equals the time premium forfeited upon exercise. But this cuts out the four bidders.

Introducing the New World Options Plan

Ever since the Financial Accounting Standards Board (FASB) and the Securities and Exchange Commission (SEC) declared that companies must theoretically value ESOs when granted and expense that theoretical value over the vesting period, there has been a very keen interest in avoiding overvaluation of the costs of ESOs to the issuer (employer). That interest has spilled over to asking questions such as, "Do employees and executives indeed perceive the options to have the same value as the company's accounting costs?"

Google's Attempt to Capture "Time Premium"

In addition to the preceding concern, another concern is that the employees really do not understand the nature and the valuation of ESOs and certainly lack knowledge of how to efficiently manage those ESOs once granted. Google introduced the concept of transferable ESOs in 2007, with the expressed motive of giving a third alternative in addition to the two alternatives of (1) hold to expiration or (2) make premature exercises and sell the stock.

> **Fast Fact**
>
> Google introduced the concept of transferable ESOs in 2007, with the expressed motive of giving a third alternative in addition to the two alternatives of (1) hold to expiration or (2) make premature exercises and sell the stock.

The company wants to allow the vested employee to "capture part, or all, of the remaining time premium" in addition to the intrinsic value. In this chapter, we offer a plan for companies to allow for their employees to capture the time premium, lower risk, enhance the value of their ESOs, and reduce taxes. Google stated, when they announced their transferables plan, that their "intent was to give employee options more tangible value" and that "the transferable options program increases the efficiency of our equity usage."

The plan is not successful. It was costly to Google and it encouraged reduction of alignment of interests.

They expected that with every transferable option that is granted the ESOs "will be more highly valued by employees," clearly suggesting that the current plans used are suboptimal for reasons we have pointed out throughout this book. Google believed, furthermore, that their ability to compete effectively for the best talent in the marketplace would be enhanced by the transferable stock options program.

In light of these new directions on the part of Google (and other companies) groping for a better solution, we present a "stock and options plan" here that is suitable for most companies. We believe it will achieve all of the expressed intents and objectives of the company but much more efficiently and with less cost to the company.

The plan we present essentially reloads to the employee the theoretical value of the time premium when the employee makes premature exercises. It also gives a further choice of converting ESOs to "restricted stock" anytime after vesting, thereby not forfeiting time premium while delaying an otherwise early tax liability.

The New World Plan

Just about every major company listed on the New York Stock Exchange and Nasdaq offers an equity compensation plan, and an estimated

11 million U.S. employees and directors own or are granted ESOs. Because of that, there is a demand for proper design of these plans that considers the grantee, and his ability to understand, value, and manage these granted securities. There clearly is a lack of plans designed where the large group of employees is given main consideration.

Objectives of the New World Plan

- To attract and retain high-quality loyal employees, officers, and directors.
- To create a continuing alignment of the interests of employees with the interests of the shareholders by granting ESOs and awarding restricted stock of the company to employees for past, present, and future performances for the company.
- To encourage employees to remain long-term, loyal, and motivated employees by using appropriate vesting schedules and mixes of equity elements.
- To promote an understanding by employees and directors of the elements and the value of such elements of the plan, and to encourage the grantee's perception of the options value at grant to equal the fair or theoretical value of the expensed costs.
- To allow for an efficient management of the employees' and directors' equity compensation by the grantee of such equity. This will be done by promoting, among other things, an understanding of the tax aspects of the receipt, vesting, and sale of the equity securities.
- To allow for an efficient management of the employees' equity compensation by incorporating various choices for the employees and directors, provided by the company, that allow for risk reduction, tax enhancement, and capture of maximum value of the equity elements, including 100 percent of the time premium of the options.
- To reduce accounting and real costs of the plan to the company.
- To enhance compliance with securities statutes and Securities and Exchange Commission (SEC) rules.
- To accomplish all of the above objects while minimizing the installation and administration costs to the company.

Elements of the New World Plan

1. The exercise price of stock options is to be equal to the average of the high and low traded prices on the day of the grant.

2. Generally, the company is to grant a mix of nonqualified stock options (these options can be "equity-settled" or "cash-settled" options) and restricted stock. The ratio of stock options to stock is to range from 2:1 to 5:1, which is at the discretion of the company. The combination of ESOs and restricted stock is less risky for the employee than 100 percent ESOs. The combination results in better alignment of interests and better tax consequences for the employee than 100 percent restricted stock grants.

3. The company will use a vesting period of two to four years (at the discretion of the company) for options and restricted stock. Shorter vesting gives more flexibility to employees. Longer vesting forces longevity of alignments.

4. There are to be at least 14 months between the grant dates of any options or restricted shares to any persons or entities subject to Section 16b of the Securities Exchange Act of 1934 and rules promulgated thereunder. The purpose of this provision is to accommodate efficient dispositions of equity securities or underlying derivatives held and to be in compliance with Section 16b.

5. Allow the grantee the right to exchange, anytime after vesting, his nonqualified options for restricted stock (with a new two-year vesting period). This is what Steve Jobs of Apple Computer did in 2003. This allows the employee to reduce risk. It also gives the employee a clearer perception of the value of the ESOs. The company is to grant a reload of the ESOs upon exercise of options equal to the value of the "time premium" forfeited to the company. The exercise price of the reloaded new ESOs is to be the average market price on the day of reload grant. The maximum contractual time to expiration is to be ten years from the grant day, unless termination comes earlier. Alternatively, if the employer wishes to assure longer alignment, it can make the ESOs settle in securities or cash for 75 percent of the intrinsic value and have the other 25 percent be reloaded back to the exercising employee in time premium as above in addition to the reload of the otherwise forfeited time premium.

These choices and features in the NWP eliminate the need to ever forfeit any time premium and thus adds value to the options. These choices are the most important elements of the plan.

6. Calculations of the fair value of the options exchanged for restricted stock and time premium forfeited upon early exercise are done by the company consistent with the assumptions used to calculate fair value for expense purposes. Any disputes vis-à-vis theoretical calculations are to be determined by the company only.

7. All obligations of the company to allow exchanges of options for restricted stock and to reload prematurely exercised ESOs are ended upon termination of employment other than upon retirement.

8. Company will report quarterly to the grantee the total "deltas" (i.e., stock equivalent positions) of all his equity holdings together with their theoretical value, using standard theoretical models with appropriate assumptions. The company will also report quarterly the daily erosion of time premium of the employees' derivative positions.

9. Company will automatically exercise the options that are in-the-money by more than 1 point (or some appropriate percentage) if the options are not exercised on or before the expiration day. Upon automatic exercise, the company will pay the former owners of the ESOs cash (after withholding proper taxes required) equal to the intrinsic value of the options on expiration day using the average price of the stock on that day. This provision does not extend the life of options held by terminated employees or directors that have otherwise been reduced by termination.

10. This paragraph applies only to officers and directors who are subject to Section 16b of the Securities Exchange Act of 1934. Company to disallow any transactions in any equity securities of the company within six months after the grant of ESOs or award of restricted stock if the market price is higher than the market price of stock on the latest grant or award day, the consequence of which will be a reduction of the total long deltas of the grantee's position.

11. Company to make a reasonable effort to communicate the terms and definitions of the plan to all participants.

How the New World Plan Achieves Results

The nature of employee stock options, as well as the value, and the proper ways to manage those employee stock options by the grantee are rarely well understood by the employee, officer, or director or their financial advisers. Part of this design requires the company to teach those employees about the nature and value of ESOs, and the proper management of their equity compensation. After the company has communicated to the employees, officers, and directors a better understanding, these employees, officers, and directors will then be able to understand their choices and maximize the value of the equity compensation, reduce risk, and lower or delay taxes.

The design of the New World Plan will give the employees, officers, and directors choices that are not available in other plans. These choices allow the reduction of risks. Holding naked ESOs involves substantial speculative risks. ESOs, especially at-the-money and out-of-the-money ESOs, lose value if the stock goes down, if the stock stays the same, or if the stock even moves up slightly. This design allows the grantee to reduce risk by exchanging his highly speculative ESOs, after vesting for less risky restricted stock, which he can later sell and is practically assured of some return.

The design of the New World Plan also allows the employee, officer, or director to capture 100 percent of the time premium immediately after vesting, either through the exchange of options for restricted stock or by premature exercises of in-the-money ESOs, whereby the company returns to the grantee the forfeited time premium. This is the most efficient way for the employee to capture the time premium. Of course, the employee could still "write" slightly out-of-the-money long-term calls as a hedge against holding ESOs and thus capture time premium.

The methods described in the New World Plan help employees, officers, and directors to retain their maximum alignment with the shareholders, while at the same time reducing risk and achieving some cash prior to the full term of the options.

The New World Plan choices also make the options grant more valuable to employees, officers, and directors, thereby allowing the company to reduce the numbers of options granted and the accounting costs of such grants. The Plan allows for a more accurate valuation of the ESOs for all purposes because these granted ESOs are more similar to listed calls than other options of plans with fewer choices. This plan eliminates the concern that the options may be unexercised, with the grantee losing value when the options are in-the-money at expiration day. It also helps the company to hire and hold the best employees because the employees will know that their interests are more protected than with other plans.

Now, we offer a comparison of a few other general options plans and exit strategies to help illustrate why the New World Plan we are proposing is superior to what is out there right now.

Below is a comparison of five ways of managing ESO risks.

- Strategy 1: Premature exercises and sales of stock as anticipated in a typical stock option plan.
- Strategy 2: Selling to Morgan institutional bidders with the Google transferable type plan.
- Strategy 3: Holding unhedged options to expiration.
- Strategy 4: Avoiding premature exercises and writing out-of-the-money two-year calls.
- Strategy 5: Our New World Options and Restricted Stock Plan.

Example
Assumptions
Google: Employee has vested options to buy 1,000 shares
Market price: $450
Exercise price: $250
Assumed expected volatility: .29
Expected time to expiration: 4 years (maximum time: 5 years)
Interest rate: 5 percent; dividend: 0
Market value of two-year calls with strike price $470 = $84 each
Theoretical value of ESOs with $250 exercise price = Black-Scholes
Theoretical value of $251,450 = ($200,000 intrinsic value + $51,450 time premium)

Comparing the Five Strategies

- Strategy 1: Premature exercise and sale at price of $450.

  Results: Net proceeds after 40 percent tax = $120,000 with no future taxes due.

- Strategy 2: Selling to Morgan/Google with stock at $450.

  Results: Net proceeds after 40 percent tax = $120,000 + some time premium attached to the sale = approximately $132,000 with no future taxes due.

- Strategy 3: Holding unhedged options to expiration.

  Hold in-the-money ESOs naked to expiration. Value of ESOs is $251,450 at present with no tax having been paid and no time premium forfeited. This strategy is highest risk and highest potential reward. Results depend on value of stock at expiration.

- Strategy 4: Selling ("writing") listed out-of-the-money long-term calls.

  Results depend on price of stock at expiration of two-year call options written: Stock at $300 would yield a profit on naked calls of $84,000 before taxes, plus theoretical value of ESOs (i.e., $96,400 of theoretical value). Opportunity to make another sale of two-year calls prior to expiration of ESOs. If stock is at $500, this would yield a profit on naked call writes of $54,000 before tax. The theoretical value of ESOs equals $281,000. Immediate tax equals 40 percent of $54,000. Probable tax on ESOs 2.5 years away. Opportunity to make another sale of calls with two years to expiration. Stock $800. Loss on written call: $246,000. ESOs equal $579,000. No tax paid on ESOs until exercised. Is the $246,000 tax deductibility offsetting the gain on ESOs dollar for dollar? It depends on whether the traded options are "hedging transactions" under IRS Section 1221. Probability of stock being within $300 to $800 in 4 years, starting at $450, is approximately 60 percent.

- Strategy 5: New World Plan.

  At a price of $450, the intrinsic value equals $200,000 on the Google ESOs. Time premium equals $51,450, which is returned to ESO grantee as a reload upon exercise. The reload has a new ten-year expiration and market exercise price. Tax on $200,000 is $80,000. Therefore, the grantee receives $120,000 net from the intrinsic value plus time premium of $51,450. Total value = $171,450. This plan allows 75 percent of the intrinsic value to be paid at exercise in cash and 25% in value as a reload of ESOs plus the otherwise forfeited time premium as a reload. The total equals

		EXHIBIT 20.1	**Strategy Matrix**	
Strategy Number	Stock Price	ESO Time Remaining	Fair Value Before Tax	Net Proceeds After Tax
1	$450	4 expected years	$251,450	$120,000
2	$450	4 expected years	$251,450	$132,000
3	$450	4 expected years	$251,450	Unknown[a]
4	$450	4 expected years	$251,450	Unknown[a]
5	$450	4 expected years	$251,450	$171,450[b]
6	$450	4 expected years	$251,450	$191,450[b]

[a]Expected value minus tax at expiration.
[b]Not considering prospective tax on the time premium reloaded.

$90,000 cash after tax plus time premium equal to $101,450. This alternative is for the employer who wishes the employees to maintain more alignment and longevity, while still pulling down substantial cash amounts while forfeiting less time premium. The theoretical value of the initial grant should be lower than in the basic New World Plan and result in a lower cost to the employer (see Exhibit 20.1).

Conclusion

The New World Plan, in addition to allowing grantees to capture 100 percent of the time premium embodied in ESOs at time of grant, also facilitates reducing risk and potential tax liability. It also serves the interest of the company by extending the alignment of interests for longer periods. It goes a long way toward eliminating the difference between the fair value expense and the real or perceived value that the grantee receives.

21

Understanding
Executive Abuses I

An unfortunate example of backdating can be found when reviewing the case of William Sorin, former general counsel for Comverse Technology, Inc., and CEO Kobi Alexander.

Backdating

William Sorin, general counsel for Comverse, and Kobi Alexander were accused by the Securities and Exchange Commission (SEC) and the New York attorney general of fraud in their backdating activities. They were accused of fraud for changing the dates of the grants to a day when the stock was lower in order to have a lower exercise price. This makes the ESOs much more valuable.

Sorin paid a $3 million fine and copped a plea on one count. At the time this book went to production, Alexander was hiding in Nambia trying to avoid extradition, taking over $100 million away with him when he fled the United States. The specifics of this backdating case were detailed

> **Backdating**
>
> An illegal practice carried out by executives who seek to extract excessive gains from the company they work for. It involves issuing employee stock options with exercise prices lower than they should be. They do so by choosing an earlier day as the grant day when the stock was lower.

recently in an SEC litigation release. It completely sheds light on the activities by Alexander, Sorin, and David Kreinberg.

The Release

According to an SEC litigation release from January 10, 2007, the SEC settled this options backdating case against the defendant, William Sorin. In particular, "the SEC settled the civil charges against William F. Sorin, the former General Counsel of Comverse Technology, Inc., and other executives arising from an alleged scheme to backdate stock option grants.

The SEC charged Sorin and the other executives on August 9, 2006, with "engaging over many years in a fraudulent scheme to grant undisclosed in-the-money options to themselves and to others by backdating stock option grants to coincide with historically low closing prices of Comverse common stock." Among other charges, the SEC alleged that Sorin actually created company records that "falsely indicated that Comverse's compensation committee had approved a grant of stock options on a date when, in reality, no such corporate action took place." Making matters worse, Sorin was charged with falsification of company records that helped in a similar backdating scheme at Ulticom, Inc., a public majority-owned subsidiary of Comverse.

Sorin, however, did not admit or deny the SEC allegations. He was required to pay $1,670,915 in "disgorgement," $1,007,201 of which represented the "in-the-money" benefit from exercises of backdated option grants. He is also required to pay $817,509 in prejudgment interest thereon, and a $600,000 civil penalty, for a total of $3,088,424.

Sorin consented to the entry of an order permanently prohibiting him from acting as an officer or director of any issuer that has a class of securities registered pursuant to Section 12 of the Securities Exchange Act of 1934 or that is required to file reports pursuant to Section 15(d) of the act. The settlement, which included barring Sorin from practicing before the SEC as an attorney among other rulings, was approved by the United States District Court for the Eastern District of New York.

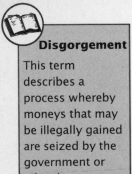

Disgorgement

This term describes a process whereby moneys that may be illegally gained are seized by the government or taken by court order from the holder of alleged illegal profits.

Spring-Loading and Manipulation

Another example of executive abuse of stock options occurred in the case of top executives of J.P. Morgan on January 20, 2009, when millions of Stock Appreciation Rights (SARS) were granted on the day that the stock hit its low price for five years. J.P. Morgan is the recipient of at least $80 billion of U.S. tax payer bail-out money. Their grants totaled nearly $50 million to the top five executives at J.P. Morgan, the value of which has more than doubled on August 1, 2009.

Just today, September 25, 2009, we are reading about an extraordinary story of Marvel Entertainment CEO Isaac "Ike" Perlmutter receiving mega grants (1,270,000) of stock options with exercise prices far below the apparently expected bid prices from Disney now at 100 percent higher than the options grant prices.

See link below:

www.ft.com/cms/s/0/233a471a-a96c-11de-9b7f-00144feabdc0.html

Conclusion

As these and the other abuse cases make clear, there appear to be many opportunities for owners or officers to find ways to make easy money.

Chapter

Understanding Executive Abuses II

Until just recently, we were puzzled as to why highly intelligent executives would make substantially "premature" exercises of their executive stock options and immediately sell the stock. Although they rarely understand the full nature of ESOs, executives can afford to hire experts to advise them on the proper management of their portfolios of employer securities. No genuine expert would advise executives to make substantially premature exercises of long-term ESOs, especially since there are viable hedging strategies available.

Did You Know?

No genuine expert would advise executives to make substantially premature exercises of long-term ESOs, especially since there are viable hedging strategies available.

Disguised Reloading

The time premium forfeited and the current tax liability incurred upon early exercise are penalties that are necessary only in rare circumstances. The risk reduction of diversifying does not justify the costs of premature exercise and sale. So, is there another reason that executives make premature exercises that is not apparent? The answer is yes. We call it disguised reloading.

Disguised Reloading

This is the process of compensation committees granting new executive stock options (ESOs) to favored executives to replace older ESOs that were recently exercised and the stock was sold. The pretention is that since the executive has lost some of his alignment through the exercise and stock sale from earlier granted options, he should be reloaded with a new round of ESOs. But in this case the reload provision is not mentioned in the executive's employment contract but is granted at the discretion of the compensation committee.

Traditional Reload Provisions

In the past, some grants of employee stock options had a provision that upon exercise and sale of the received stock, the grantee would automatically receive another similar load of employee stock options. These new options would have the strike price at the current market and a new ten years of time remaining. Assume, for example, the grantee was granted 1 million options to buy stock at $20 for the next 10 years. Assume that the stock had an expected volatility of .41. Assume also that the stock advanced to $40 after three years and the executive exercised his ESOs and sold the stock received. He would get approximately 60 percent of the intrinsic value after tax or about $12 million.

How much time premium would he have forfeited back to the company? To get the answer, we merely calculate the theoretical value of the ESOs immediately prior to exercise and subtract the intrinsic value from the theoretical value. The theoretical value is about $25.1 million, with the intrinsic value of $20 million. This makes the forfeited time premium equal to $5.1 million. But the reload feature gives the executive 1 million new ESOs with a strike price of $40, with the stock at $40 and with maximum ten years to expiration day. The question becomes: "What is the value of the new options?"

Well, the theoretical value is $18 million. That is more than enough to pay the executive for the forfeited time premium of $5.1 million plus the tax paid of $8 million. But stockholders have become wary of reload clauses because of their abusive characteristics.

Reload clauses are now rarely part of the options contract. However, nothing stops the compensation committee from reloading the executive with 1 million new ESOs with a strike price of $40, whether the reload provision is in the contract or not. The reload is justified to maintain the alignment or so it is said.

Accounting Costs

Let's take a look at the accounting costs associated with the preceding scenario. The fair value of the options granted with an exercise price and a current market price of $20 is about $9 million. The fair value of the options granted at $40 is $18 million. So the expenses against earnings for the grant and the reload are $27 million.

The $5.1 million that is forfeited back to the company is not even considered a reduction of accounting expenses.

Now let's analyze the extra cost to the company of the disguised reload. It is essentially $13 million since the $5.1 million is in reality forfeited back to the company. But the extra accounting cost is $18 million because, for accounting purposes, the $5.1 million is not counted.

Compared with Backdating

Let's compare this scenario to backdating of the 1 million shares. Assume that the true market value of the stock was $30, but the grant day was backdated to the time when the stock was $20. Assume the same volatility and expected time to expiration (i.e., .41 and 6.5 years respectively).

1. Fair value of the 1 million ESOs with a strike and market price of $20 is $9 million.
2. Fair value of the 1 million ESOs with a strike and market price of $30 is $13.5 million, making the difference $4.5 million (i.e., $13.5 million – $9 million = $4.5 million).
3. Fair value of the 1 million ESOs with a strike price of $20 and a market price of the stock of $30 is $16 million, making the difference $3.5 million ($17 million – $13.5 million = $3.5 million).

This disguised reload in this comparison is 4 to 5 times more costly to a company in real terms than a very large case of backdating.

The cost to the company is 5 to 8 times as great in accounting terms. Disguised reloads are much more frequent and much more costly and are therefore much more abusive than backdating.

Conclusion

This is where the real money is bagged. Maybe the shareholders will wake up to this scam, which is far bigger than backdating. But when these executives add disguised reloads on top of backdating or spring-loading, it is easy to see why much of the company's earnings are going to the top executives.

Chapter 23

Understanding Executive Abuses III

Pumping and Dumping

In this chapter, we send you on a pumping and dumping journey with Mr. Lucky.

Mr. Lucky Goes to Yahoo!

Mr. Lucky was granted employee stock options (ESOs) when he went to work for Yahoo! on April 16, 2001. The stock was trading at $17.61. However, he did not start as CEO and Chairman until May 1, 2001 when the stock was $22.10. Could it be that Mr. Lucky was really granted those options on May 1, 2001, and they were backdated to a day when the stock was $4.5 lower? The stock was at $17.61, and he received a total of 10 million ESOs to buy stock at prices as indicated here:

> 5 million at $17.61
> 2.5 million at $30
> 1.5 million at $60
> 1 million at $75

Total: 10 million.

Approximate value: $100 million

The fair value of the preceding options was approximately $100 million at grant time. Perhaps this was the largest bonus ever paid to attract a CEO to a job. But why was not May 1, 2001, the day of the grant? It was the day he became CEO and chairman.

Looks Suspicious

After five and one half months, Yahoo! stock was down to $9.24. On October 2, 2001, Mr. Lucky was granted another million ESOs with a $9.24 exercise price; fair value was about $6 million. With the stock about $12.92 on July 11, 2002, Mr. Lucky received a mere 2 million ESOs to buy the stock at $12.92 and another 800,000 at $16.46 on December 12, 2002. The combined theoretical value was $20.5 million for a bonus given for a job well done. After all, the stock was only down 45 percent since he started as CEO 20 months earlier (or down 30 percent from the day of the $100 million grant).

Lucky Time

But things changed and Mr. Lucky started to get lucky. He begins to cash in on some of those options and duly exercises 500,000 ESOs with eight years to expiration (the only case we have seen of exercising with eight years to go). He then sells the stock at prices between $32 and $32.64 in 19 different trades. He nets $23.10 ($32.34 − $9.24) on 437,500 shares equal to $10,106,250, plus $15.90 on 62,500 shares equal to $993,750.

Total gain: $11,096,000

On October 14, 2003, Mr. Lucky is back exercising ESOs prematurely and selling stock. He exercises 333,334 shares with a strike price of

$12.92 and sells the stock between $42.31 and $42.70. On the same day, he also exercises 62,500 of his $9.24 ESOs and 104,166 exercisable at $16.46 with an average of seven years remaining on the options. His net looks as follows:

$$\$29.60 \times 333,334 = \$9,866,686 \text{ plus}$$
$$\$33.25 \times 62,500 \quad = \$2,078,125 \text{ plus}$$
$$\$26.06 \times 104,166 = \$2,714,565$$

Total gain: $ 14,659,376

Mr. Lucky then exercises and sells 63,200 ESOs with a strike price of $9.24 and sells at $48 on February 12, 2004. Range of the stock: $47.23 to $48.07.

Total gain: $2,449,632.

If you thought he was lucky, now the real luck begins. On March 10, 2004, or thereabouts, Mr. Lucky is granted 2.9 million ESOs with an exercise price of $41.70 (five cents higher than the lowest close of 2004—it would look bad if he got the absolute low). On April 7, 2004, Yahoo! announces record earnings and a 2:1 split of the stock. The stock moved up before the news to $48. Perhaps Mr. Lucky spread the news to other insiders so they could be lucky, too. Yahoo! opened after the news at $56 and change.

On April 12, Mr. Lucky exercised 1.5 million ESOs with strike prices of $9.24, $12.92, and $16.46, with perhaps 5.5 years to go, and sells some size stock at the lucky prices of $54.88 to $55.65.

Total gain: $60 million jackpot.

On April 15 and 16, 2004, Mr. Lucky exercises another 500,000 ESOs and sells stock between $54.29 and $54.70: $3,262, 616 + $5,219, 773.

Total gain: $8,482,389.

On July 13, 2004, Mr. Lucky exercises a total of 1,632,500 ESOs with strike prices of $4.62, $6.46, $8.23, and $8.81. These exercise prices were adjusted for the split.

Total gain: $37,002,425.

Mr. Lucky then exercises 367,500 ESOs on July 14, 2004, at $8.81 and sells at prices ranging between $30.45 and $30.58.
Total gain: $7,974,750.

Mr. Lucky exercises another 1 million ESOs at $8.81 and sells at between $29.85 and $30.05 on July 27, 2004.
Total gain: $21,140,000.

Lucky is at it again. On October 19, 2004, he exercises 900,000 ESOs at $4.62, $8.23, and at $8.81 and sells at between $35 and $35.53. Stock closes at $34.64.
Total gain: $24,394,500.

On October 20, 2004, Mr. Lucky exercises 167,000 ESOs and sells at an average $34.35.
Total gain: $4,265,180.

Mr. Lucky goes on exercising and selling again: 1,383,000 at 8.81. He gets prices from $35.10 to $35.80 on October 21, 2004.
Total gain: $36,856,950.

On October 22, 2004, Mr. Lucky exercises 550,000 at 8.81 and sells for between $35.60 and $36.60.
Total gain: $15,009,500.

Mr. Lucky gets a bonus grant of 1.4 million ESOs with a strike price of $37.08 on December 16, 2004.
Theoretical value of ESOs: $23,360,040.

On January 24, 2005, 34,500 ESOs are exercised but no stock is sold. Lucky must have a reason for not selling.

On February 1, 2005, Mr. Lucky is granted 2 million ESOs at $34.75 per share.
Theoretical value of ESOs granted: $29,000,000.

On February 4, 2005, Mr. Lucky exercises at $4.62 and sells 23,900 shares at $35.09 to $35.23.
Total gain: $729,906.

On April 22, 2005, Mr. Lucky exercises 880,000 ESOs and sells stock at various prices between $34.87 and $35.31.
Total gain: $24,189,759.

On April 25, 2005, Mr. Lucky exercises prematurely 620,000 ESOs at $8.81 and sells stock between $34.67 and $35.
Total gain: $16,132,40.

On April 27, 2005, Mr. Lucky exercises 200,000 ESOs at $8.81 and receives sales of stock at $35 and $35.10.
Total gain: $5,248,000.

On May 4, 2005, Mr. Lucky exercises 750,000 ESOs with a strike price of $8.81 and sells stock at $35.15 to $35.45.
Total gain: $19,867,500.

On August 19, 2005, Mr. Lucky is again exercising options with strike prices of $4.62, $8.23, and $8.81 and selling stock at prices from $34.23 to $34.45. His total exercise and sales are 542,886.
Total gain: $14,053,500.

On October 24, 2005, Mr. Lucky cashes in by selling stock he received from exercising options to buy 66,667 at $8.23, 763,149 at $8.81 and 83,334 at $4.62.
Total gain: $24,485,863.

On October 25, 2005, Mr. Lucky exercises 534,921 ESOs at $15 and 104,297 at $8.81 and sells stock at prices between $35.10 and $35.31.
Total gain: $13,557,801.

On October 26, 2005, Mr. Lucky is exercising 447,632 ESOs at $15 and sells stock at prices between $35.05 and $35.58.
Total gain: $9,091,405.

On October 27, 2005, Mr. Lucky exercises 500,000 ESOs with an exercise price of $15 and sells stock at between $35.40 and $35.45.
Total gain: $10,201,000.

On October 28, 2005, another 500,000 ESOs with strike price of $15 are exercised. The stock goes at prices between $35.43 and $35.80.
Total gain: $10,295,000.

On February 15, 2006, Mr. Lucky is still getting lucky as he unloads 266,667 more ESOs. The exercise price is $15. And he exercises 133,333 more ESOs with an exercise price of $8.23. He sells the stock at market prices between $33.03 and $33.32.
Total gain: $8,170,664.

On February 16 and 17, 2006, 300,000 ESOs are disposed of by exercise (strike price $15). Stock is sold at prices from $33.05 to $33.25.
Total gain: $5,445,000.

On February 21 and 22, 2006, 300,000 ESOs with a strike price of $15 are exercised and the stock is sold at prices from $33.03 to $33.10.
Total gain: $5,418,000.

Final Total Gain

Total gains before tax on options exercises and stock sales is $421 million as of July 4, 2006. This does not include the value of options granted but not exercised, and does not include restricted stock received either sold or held (estimated at $350 million to $450 million in addition to the $421 million).

On March 10, 2006, Mr. Lucky is granted ESOs to purchase 1.3 million shares of stock at $40.68. Fair value: $11 million. The purpose of this grant is unknown. The stock was trading at $30.58 at the close on March 10, 2006. Why grant a bonus worth $11 million when the March 10, 2004, bonus was for 900,000 shares at $41.70 when the stock was trading at $41.70. The theoretical value of those 900,000 options was almost $19 million at grant day.

Mr. Lucky then gets really lucky on May 31, 2006, when he is granted 6 million ESOs to buy the stock at market value of $31.59. The theoretical value is near $67 million to $71 million at grant day. Is there something coming at the upcoming earnings announcements to make the stock jump? We will watch it. Or maybe this story will break and Yahoo! and Mr. Lucky will have some explaining to do.

I predict that Mr. Lucky will have some papers delivered to him that may make him feel a bit unlucky. He also may be feeling a bit unlucky after Yahoo! tumbled $6.5 on July 19, 2006. I predict that Mr. Lucky will go the Compensation Committee and demand more ESOs because of how much he lost today in value.

Mr. Lucky's End

Mr. Lucky actually got a bit unlucky in May 2007 when five law firms sued him for fraud and misrepresentation in an alleged "pump and dump" scheme, beginning in April 2004, and presented in this chapter as an example of pumping and dumping.

IRS Tax Implications of Hedging ESOs under IRS Sections: 1221, 1259, 1091, 1092

The rules governing taxes that apply to hedging assets with derivatives such as puts and calls are quite complicated. The fact that the main assets we are interested in are nonqualified ESOs, which have features of securities (similar to call options) and ordinary assets (the gain from ESO contracts are considered compensation income, never capital gains), makes it even more complicated.

In this section we explain in detail the following tax concepts and rules that play a role in hedging against ESOs and stock using listed calls and puts. The title sections and their corresponding URLs are:

Substantially identical securities: IRS Publication 550 (2008)
www.irs.gov/publications/p550/index.html
Constructive Sale: IRS, Section 1259
www.taxalmanac.org/index.php/Sec._1259

Wash Sale: IRS, Section 1091

www.taxalmanac.org/index.php/Internal_Revenue_Code:Sec._1091._
Loss_from_wash_sales_of_stock_or_securities

Hedging transaction: IRS, Section 1221

www.taxalmanac.org/index.php/Sec._1221

Straddle: IRS, Sect. 1092; identified straddle: 1092(a)(2)

www.taxalmanac.org/index.php/Internal_Revenue_Code:Sec._1092._
Straddles

Substantially Identical Securities

The following definition of substantially identical stock or securities is taken
from IRS Publication 550 (2008). This definition is relevant especially to
the Wash Sale (Section 1091) and the Constructive Sale (Section 1259).

> In determining whether stock or securities are substantially
> identical, you must consider all the facts and circumstances in
> your particular case. Ordinarily, stocks or securities of one cor-
> poration are not considered substantially identical to stocks or
> securities of another corporation. However, they may be sub-
> stantially identical in some cases. For example, in a reorganiza-
> tion, the stocks and securities of the predecessor and successor
> corporations may be substantially identical.
>
> Similarly, bonds or preferred stock of a corporation are not or-
> dinarily considered substantially identical to the common stock
> of the same corporation. However, where the bonds or preferred
> stock are convertible into common stock of the same corpora-
> tion, the relative values, price changes, and other circumstances
> may make these bonds or preferred stock and the common stock
> substantially identical. For example, preferred stock is substan-
> tially identical to the common stock if the preferred stock:
> • Is convertible into common stock,
> • Has the same voting rights as the common stock,
> • Is subject to the same dividend restrictions,
> • Trades at prices that do not vary significantly from the conversion
>   ratio, and
> • Is unrestricted as to convertibility.

The preceding is from IRS Publication 550 (2008) and refers to convertible preferred stock's being "substantially identical" to common stock under some conditions. It is helpful in our analysis of the Wash Sale and Constructive Sale application to listed and employee stock options, as the references say that if all of the five conditions apply, there is a "substantially identical" security.

For example, the statement that the preferred "trades at prices that do not vary significantly from the conversion ratio" means that if the stock moves up one point, the preferred moves up the same amount that would reflect the number of shares the preferred holder would receive on conversion. To say it another way for the more options-experienced readers, the latent warrants contained within the convertible preferred stock must have a delta that approached 1.00. Had IRS Publication 550 said the convertible preferred "trades at prices that reflect a part of the conversion ratio," we would have to say that perhaps a call option with a .60 delta may be considered substantially identical to the stock.

So IRS Publication 550 essentially says that for options to be substantially identical to the stock, they must trade at prices that do not vary significantly from their intrinsic value.

This would imply that a call with significantly less delta than 1.00 would not be "substantially identical" with the stock, nor would the sale of puts with a delta of .60 be "substantially identical" to the purchase of stock.

The next excerpt from the Chicago Board Options Exchange (**CBOE**) tax page lends support to our view as to the definition of "substantially identical":

> The "substantially identical" test requires that the securities be of the same issuer and be commercially identical in all major respects, including interest rate, maturity date, dividend provisions, liquidating preferences and other similar priorities. If the instruments are virtually similar or identical, the overriding test is whether or not the marketplace views them as such, i.e., whether or not movement of one security correlates to the price movement of the other security. Thus, if a graph of relative price movements produces parallel lines, the securities are generally substantially identical. If such a result does not occur, they are not substantially identical.

So with the definitions of "substantially identical" explained here, we proceed with the discussion of the Constructive Sale and Wash Sale Rules.

Constructive Sale

Constructive Sale means that a sale for tax purposes takes place when a person holds stocks, options, or ESOs and makes a transaction that is "substantially identical" with a direct sale of the security held. It also applies if a person is short a security and then buys a security that is "substantially identical" with the security shorted.

For example, he may be long 1,000 shares of Exxon and sells ten near-term deep-in-the-money calls with .95 deltas. The sale of the ten calls is "substantially identically" to a sale of the stock and is a Constructive Sale. It is possible that options that are near-term and have a .90 delta are sold, this could be construed as a sale of a "substantially identical" security.

More examples of Constructive Sales are sales of single stock futures, purchases of deep-in-the-money puts, or synthetic sales of stock using simultaneous sales of calls and purchases of puts with the same exercise price and time to expiration.

If he sold ten calls with a .60 delta and two years to expiration, on the 1,000 shares of Exxon stock, that transaction could not reasonably be considered a Constructive Sale.

Another example is: assume a person shorted 100,000 shares of Bank of America at $40. Assume also that three years later he bought 1,000 long-term equity anticipation securities (LEAPS) calls with .60 deltas each when the stock was trading at $10. The calls had 18 months to expiration when purchased. The purchase of the 1,000 calls would not be considered a purchase of a "substantially identical" security, and the Constructive Sale Rule would not apply.

Wash Sale

Wash Sale means a sale of a security at a loss together with the purchase of a "substantially identical" security or with a purchase of an option to buy a "substantially identical" security made within a period 30 days before or 30 days after the sale of the security. This means that if a person buys 100 shares of stock at $50 and later sell the 100 shares at $25, the losing sale will be a Wash Sale if during the 61-day period around the sale at $25, the exact stock or a "substantially identical" security or a call on the same stock is purchased.

So even if he buys an out-of-the-money call within the 61-day period of the losing sale, the sale is a Wash Sale and the deduction is disallowed currently. This is so because the rule specifically says so.

However, assume a person buys a call at $10. Later he sells the call at $7 and simultaneously buys a call with a different exercise price and substantially longer time remaining to expiration.

The risk factors, such as the risks from delta, gamma, theta, and vega associated with owning calls with a shorter expiration date and different exercise prices can be—and most cases are—far different from owning calls with substantially longer time to expiration and with different exercise prices.

No reasonable person would argue that the purchase of a call with substantially longer time remaining and with different exercise prices would be a purchase of a "substantially identical" security to a call sold with shorter time remaining and a substantially different exercise price.

Assume he writes a call at $15 and later buys it back at $25 after the stock has advanced, and 10 days later sells two different calls with a substantially higher exercise price and longer time to expiration. This would not be a Wash Sale and the deduction of the $1,000 loss would be usable currently. The risks of changing one short call position to two calls short with perhaps half the delta of the single call is significant. This is so because a large up move would give a much larger loss with the two calls short than the one call short. However, a small up move would make one position show a gain and the other a loss. No informed person would claim that the two positions are "substantially identical".

Identified Hedging Transaction

The following language is taken from IRS Regs. Section 1.1221-2 and gives a definition of a "hedging transaction". Essentially, it says that if transactions are made to manage the risk of holding ordinary property, the gains or losses are ordinary.

Identified Hedge under IRS Regs. Section 1.1221-2

(b) Hedging transaction defined. Section 1221(b)(2)(A) provides that a hedging transaction is any transaction that a taxpayer enters into in the normal course of the taxpayer's trade or business primarily—

(1) To manage risk of price changes or currency fluctuations with respect to ordinary property (as defined in paragraph (c)(2) of this section) that is held or to be held by the taxpayer;

(2) To manage risk of interest rate or price changes or currency fluctuations with respect to borrowings made or to be made, or ordinary obligations incurred or to be incurred, by the taxpayer; or

(3) To manage such other risks as the Secretary may prescribe in regulations (see paragraph (d)(6) of this section).

As an example: assume that an executive, as one of the top executives of J.P. Morgan, was granted 700,000 nonqualified ESOs on J.P. Morgan stock with a strike price of $19.49 on January 20, 2009, which is trading at $35 on May 21, 2009. He wished to hedge the position somewhat, and buys 5,000 of the 14-month puts with an exercise price of $40. Prior to the trade, he recorded the transaction as a "hedging transaction." The transaction reduces delta risk but increases theta and vega risk. He also sold 5000 puts with a strike price of $20. Assume the stock trades at $50 when the puts expire. The entire loss on the puts bought is currently deductible as an ordinary loss, if the hedge is accepted as a "hedging transaction" under Section 1221.

The Straddle Rule would not apply, in our view, because it is designed to address offsetting positions in capital assets, which are regularly traded. While it is true that the puts are capital assets, the nonqualified ESOs are not capital assets. Any ordinary property that is subject to a "hedging transaction" as defined in IRS Regs. Section 1.1221-2, is not considered a capital asset as capital asset is defined in Regs. Section 1.1221-2.

But Section 1092 (d) (1) defines the term personal property as meaning any personal property of a type that is actively traded. ESOs, whether qualified or not, generally, as a matter of contract with the company, cannot be actively traded. It, therefore, would be very hard to claim that ESOs are actively traded.

However, Section 1092(d)(2) defines position as including an interest (including an option) in personal property. So these definitions suggest that an option that is not actively traded on stock that is actively traded could be included in a straddle. In my view, the word *option* here was intended to be an option that is actively traded.

Even if the straddle rule did apply, there would be no "fair market value" of the ESOs to determine the unrecognized gain on the ESOs, and there would be no requirement to report the unrecognized gain under Section 1092 para. 3(c)(ii)(II). See below.

IRS, Section 1092(a)

(3) Unrecognized gain

For purposes of this subsection—

(A) In general

The term "unrecognized gain" means—

(i) in the case of any position held by the taxpayer as of the close of the taxable year, the amount of gain which would be taken into account with respect to such position if such position were sold on the last business day of such taxable year at its fair market value, and

(ii) in the case of any position with respect to which, as of the close of the taxable year, gain has been realized but not recognized, the amount of gain so realized.

(B) Special rule for identified straddles

For purposes of paragraph (2)(A)(ii), the unrecognized gain with respect to any identified offsetting position shall be the excess of the fair market value of the position at the time of the determination over the fair market value of the position at the time the taxpayer identified the position as a position in an identified straddle.

(C) Reporting of gain

(i) In general each taxpayer shall disclose to the Secretary, at such time and in such manner and form as the Secretary may prescribe by regulations—

(I) each position (whether or not part of a straddle) with respect to which, as of the close of the taxable year, there is unrecognized gain, and

(II) the amount of such unrecognized gain.

(ii) Reports not required in certain cases

Clause (i) shall not apply—

(I) to any position which is part of an identified straddle,

(II) to any position which, with respect to the taxpayer, is property described in paragraph (1) or (2) of Section 1221 (a) or to any position which is part of a "hedging transaction" (as defined in section 1256 (e))

(III) with respect to any taxable year if no loss on a position (including a regulated futures contract) has been sustained during such taxable year or if the only loss sustained on such position is a loss described in subclause (II).

The fact that there can never be a fair market value of the ESOs since the ESOs cannot be sold or transferred, precludes the characterization of "hedging transactions" on ESOs being included under Section 1092 (the straddle rule), in our view.

Straddle IRS, Section 1092

This Section says that a person cannot deduct liquidated losses currently that are the result of holding offsetting positions, to the extent there are unrecognized gains on the offsetting positions.

For example, if a person buys 1,000 shares of Google at $380 and simultaneously buys ten puts with a exercise price of $400, those positions are considered a straddle. If the stock goes to $500 and the puts have a $30,000 liquidated loss, that loss is not deductible currently and must be used to offset the gain on the stock, when the stock is liquidated or used to raise the cost basis of the long stock by the amount of the loss on the puts.

If instead of buying puts, the owner of the stock sold "qualified covered calls," any loss on the sale of the calls, if liquidated, would be deductible currently as a short-term capital loss because sales of "qualified covered calls" do not constitute creating a straddle. This is so because "qualified covered calls" are exempt from being an offsetting position of a straddle. The sale of calls versus long stock would be a straddle if the calls sold were not "qualified covered calls." The purchase of puts or the sale of calls versus stock is also never a hedge under IRS 1.1221-2 since the stock is not "ordinary property" as defined in 1.1221(c)(2).

IRS, Sections 1092, 1256, and 1221

These sections' excerpts, read together, indicate that "hedging transactions" are not straddles. An article by Robert Willens (Daily Tax Report,

July 13, 2009) addressed whether ESOs were "financial positions" for Section 1259. He concluded that because the income from ESOs was compensation, the ESOs did not have a "gain."

Section 1092(e)

(e) Exception for hedging transactions

This section shall not apply in the case of any "hedging transaction" (as defined in section 1256 (e)).

Section 1256(e)

(e) Mark to market not to apply to hedging transactions

(1) Section not to apply

Subsection (a) shall not apply in the case of a hedging transaction.

(2) Definition of hedging transaction

1.1221 (b)(2)(A) Hedging Transaction   For purposes of this subsection, the term "hedging transaction" means any hedging transaction (as defined in Section 1221(b)(2)(A)) if, before the close of the day on which such transaction was entered into (or such earlier time as the Secretary may prescribe by regulations), the taxpayer clearly identifies such transaction as being a hedging transaction.

(A) In general

For purposes of this section, the term "hedging transaction" means any transaction entered into by the taxpayer in the normal course of the taxpayer's trade or business primarily—

(i) to manage risk of price changes or currency fluctuations with respect to ordinary property which is held or to be held by the taxpayer,

(ii) to manage risk of interest rate or price changes or currency fluctuations with respect to borrowings made or to be made, or ordinary obligations incurred or to be incurred, by the taxpayer, or

(iii) to manage such other risks as the Secretary may prescribe in regulations.

Identified Straddle

This is a straddle that has been clearly identified in the taxpayer's records as an "identified straddle" as provided under IRS Section 1092(a)(2) by a person who creates offsetting positions that involve holding capital positions and is doing offsetting trades. If there is a loss from any position in an identified straddle, the hedger must increase the cost basis of each of the positions that offset the loss position in the identified straddle by the amount of the liquidated loss.

For example, assume that 1,000 shares of stock are bought at $10 and the stock trades at $25 two years after the purchase. Assume that the hedger then spends $10,000 on ten puts that are in-the-money. Assume that at expiration day the puts are worthless because the stock is trading at 31. The $10,000 loss is treated as follows: The $6,000 of losses raises the cost basis of the stock by $6,000. The remaining $4,000 is considered a capital loss of $4,000 currently.

The preceding conclusions are my best understanding of the workings of the tax rules that relate to hedging stock, listed options, and ESOs. These are no guarantees that the final treatment of these types of hedges will be as I suggest.

Table of Tax Rules and Results

A: Positions Not Offsetting Other Positions
1. Long stock: Gains and losses are short term or long term, depending on whether the stock is held over one year or not.
2. Long call: Gains and losses are short term or long term, depending on whether the calls are held over one year or not.
3. Long put: Gains and losses are short term or long term, depending on whether the puts are held over one year or not.
4. Owning nonqualified ESOs: Gains are compensation income.
5. Owning qualified ESOs: Gains can be long-term capital gain or compensation income, depending on whether all qualifications to achieve qualified status are met.
6. Stock shorted: Short-term capital gains or losses when closed.
7. Calls written: Short-term capital gains or losses when closed.
8. Puts written: Short-term capital gains or losses when closed.

9. Long Puts: In a traditional IRA. Gains are tax deferred. Losses are deductible only against gains in the IRA.

10. Long Puts: In a Roth IRA. Gains are tax free. Losses are deductible only against gains in the IRA.

B. Exchange Traded Options Offsetting Stock Positions

1. Sale of "qualified covered calls" versus long stock: No taxes are due upon the opening write of a call. Positions do not create a straddle and are treated as if they were not offsetting.

2. Sale of nonqualified calls versus long stock: No taxes are due upon the write of calls unless the sale of the calls are considered a Constructive Sale of the stock. Positions create a straddle under Section 1092 and can be identified as an "identified straddle" by holder. Liquidated losses on one position raise the cost basis of the offsetting position, if the straddle is an identified straddle.

3. Purchase of puts versus long stock, both outside of an IRA: Positions are treated the same as 2 above. Positions create a straddle under Section 1092 and can be identified as an "identified straddle" by holder. Liquidated losses on one position raise the cost basis of the offsetting position if there is an identified straddle.

4. Purchase of puts inside a traditional IRA versus long stock outside of IRA: Gains on the puts are tax deferred. Losses may raise the cost basis of the offsetting stock if the position is considered as an identified straddle.

C. Exchange Traded Options Used to Offset the Holding of Employee Stock Options

1. Sale of calls versus nonqualified ESOs should be identified and accepted as a hedge under IRS Regs. Section 1.1221-(2): No tax liability is created at the time of the sale. Gain or loss on liquidated positions is ordinary gain or loss, regardless of the time held. In our view, the "hedging transactions" do not create Section 1092 straddles.

2. Sale of calls versus qualified ESOs.: No tax on sale date unless the sales are considered "substantially identical" to other securities held. Liquidated gains on listed calls are short-term capital gains. This transaction is not subject to IRS Section 1092 nor is it subject to IRS Section 1221.

3. Purchase of puts versus nonqualified ESOs are treated the same as sales of calls versus long nonqualified ESO positions as in 1 above.

    4. Purchase of puts versus qualified ESOs are not straddles under IRS section 1092 nor are they subject to IRS Section 1221.

D. Exchange traded Puts Purchased in IRAs Offsetting ESOs Outside of IRAs

    1. All gains on the puts are either tax free if purchased in a Roth IRA or tax deferred if purchased in a traditional IRA.

Applications of the Preceding Tax Rules to Real Stock and ESO Positions

Apple Computer is selling for $122.5 on May 22, 2009. An investor is holding 10,000 nonqualified ESOs to buy APPL at $60 plus 3,000 shares of unrestricted stock. The value of the ESOs is about $730,000 and the stock is worth $367,100. He decides to sell 50 January 2011 calls with an exercise price of $130 for a market price of $23 (i.e., $115,000 total). About 25 percent of the risks of holding the stock and the ESOs are eliminated.

Taxes on These Positions

1. The sales proceeds are not taxable and can be removed from the brokerage account without borrowing. No interest is required to be paid.

2. The 3,000 unrestricted shares far exceed any initial margin requirements.

3. Of the 50 calls sold, 30 would be considered "qualified covered calls" and are not subject to the Constructive Sale Rule, the Straddle Rule, or IRS Regs. Section 1.1221-2. Any gains or losses on the 30 "qualified covered calls" when closed are short-term capital gains or losses and reportable as such then.

4. The other 20 calls that are sold would, in our opinion, be considered part of an identified "hedging transaction" versus 2,000 of the nonqualified ESOs held. If the sales of the calls are identified "hedging transactions," the gains or losses on the closure of the written 20 calls are treated as ordinary income or loss when closed regardless of the value of the stock or the ESOs.

5. If the identification of a "hedging transaction" were disallowed, the gains and losses on the 20 calls sold would be short-term capital gain or loss when closed as they would still not be included in IRS Section 1092.

6. If the stock closed at $140 on the expiration day of the written calls and no trades were done subsequent to the sale of the 50 calls, the following tax consequences would apply: The position would be 2,000 shares short because the 50 written calls would be exercised and assigned to the writer. The 10,000 ESOs long would be undisturbed. There would be a long-term capital gain on the 3,000 shares used to cover 30 of the 50 calls assigned, assuming no purchases of the stock were made. There would be no tax due on the other assigned 2,000 shares that were shorted profitably, until closed.

7. If the stock closed at $110 on expiration day of the January 2011 calls, the calls are worthless and the gain on 30 "qualified covered calls" would be short-term capital gain. The gain on the other 20 calls would be ordinary income if there was an identified "hedging transaction" and a short-term capital gain if the calls were not considered part of a "hedging transaction."

Buying Puts Instead of Selling Calls

Now let us assume that puts were bought instead of selling calls to reduce risk of holding the stock and the ESOs as above in Apple Computer.

Assume that 70 January 2011 puts were purchased with an exercise price of $140 when the stock was $122.5. The cost of the puts may be $160,000. Assume the stock increased to $175 as expiration day of the puts arrived. The puts would be worthless. What is the tax treatment on the puts? The 30 puts versus the 3000 shares would be considered a straddle. and would be used to increase the cost basis of the stock, assuming the straddle was an identified straddle. If the offsetting remaining 40 puts were considered an identified "hedging transaction," the loss would be an ordinary loss. If the identified "hedging transaction" was not accepted, the entire loss on the 40 puts is short-term capital loss. There would be no taxable gain on either the stock or the ESOs currently, of course, because none have been liquidated. The unliquidated gains from May 22, 2009 would be $157,500 for the stock and about $485,000 for the ESOs.

On the other hand, if Apple went to $80 when the puts expired, the following would be the result: The 70 puts would have a value of $420,000, making a profit of $260,000. The 70 puts could be exercised, and the stock position would be short 4,000 shares. If the 3,000 shares that were owned were used to cover 3,000 shares short, there may be a capital gain or loss on the stock. The gain on the other puts that were exercised would not be reportable until the short 4,000 shares were covered.

Sales of Calls

The following is an example of sales of calls on J.P. Morgan to hedge a grantee's position of long 700,000 vested ESOs with strike price of $19.49, expiring in seven years of expected life.

Assume that JPM stock is trading at $34.41 on May 22, 2009. Assume 3,000 January 2011 calls are sold with a strike price of $38. Using a $50 volatility, the calls are valued at $760 per call, for a total of $2,280,000. The total delta risk was reduced by about 17,000 deltas or about 28 percent of the delta risk and an undetermined amount of theta and vega risk. Assume the stock goes to $50 in six months, making the written calls equal about $16.90. The total loss on the calls is $930 × 3,000 = $2,790,000. But the value of the 700,000 ESO would have advanced about $9.1 million. So under this scenario, the two positions result in a net gain of $6,310,000 gain, with a probable ordinary tax deduction of $2,790,000. If we assume that the offsetting positions are designated as a "hedging transaction," the loss on the calls is an ordinary loss deductible when the short call position is liquidated. When executives buy puts they must be mindful of SEC Rule 16 4-C.

Assume that the 3,000 calls are closed by a purchase of the 3,000 calls at $16.90. But simultaneously with the purchase of the January 2011 calls, the hedger buys 5,000 January 2012 puts with the exercise price of $50. This is not a Wash Sale, and the closing of the 3,000 January 2011 calls creates a current ordinary loss. The grantee has his deltas approximately the same as before he took the ordinary loss by buying back the 3,000 calls written. However, his gamma, theta, and vega risks are far different, making it unreasonable to claim that the positions are "substantially identical."

The new positions of long 700,000 ESOs versus long 5,000 January 2012 puts is a "hedging transaction" and is delta long about 350,000 to 400,000 combined.

Assume that one year after the purchase of the 5,000 puts the stock is trading at $15. The puts would be worth $17.5 million, giving a profit of about $12 million. If the grantee exercised the puts and stayed short, there would be no tax on the $12 million until the position is closed directly or indirectly.

Additionally, the executive would have had to comply with Sections 16b and 16c of the Securities Exchange Act of 1934 and SEC Rule C-4, which may cause the full consequences to be different from the above.

Conclusion

With all of the preceding analysis in mind, what is the best way to proceed if you believe that selling calls and/or buying puts versus ESOs reduces risks and preserves the ESOs' value and is far superior to premature exercises and sell strategies?

The answer is to identify sales of calls and purchases of puts as "hedging transactions" under Section 1221.

While there is a chance of an adverse selection against you, such that there are tax surprises, these will be minor relative to the gains that will result from avoiding premature exercises, reducing risks, and enhancing the values of your ESOs with listed calls and puts.

The best tax results and overall results will be achieved by selling out-of-the-money listed calls and buying some at-the-money puts, always maintaining substantial long deltas, especially early in the life of the equity grants. This should be followed by strategically closing loss positions followed by a rehedge with nonsubstantially identical replacements. Closing profitable positions should be delayed. Try to use IRAs and other deferred compensation plans in coordination with the hedging. Buying Vertical Put Spreads, especially in an IRA, may be the best vehicle to use to hedge ESOs considering all factors.

The views expressed in this appendix are ours, obviously. We are aware that some of them are contrary to some others in the field.

We advise checking with qualified tax advisors prior to relying on the tax ideas expressed herein.

Michael Gray (CPA, Silicon Valley) has provided very helpful insight to various tax issues. He can be reached at www.taxtrimmers.com

Did the SEC Encourage Backdating and Spring-Loading?

S ection 16b of the Securities Exchange Act of 1934 requires that any profits made by executives through purchases and sales of company equity securities within six months be recoverable by the company. Please visit: www.law.uc.edu/CCL/34Act/sec16.html to view this section.

Prior to 1991, the "grant" of an employee stock option (ESO) was not considered a purchase for Section 16b "short swing" purposes. Nor was the grant considered as part of matched trades for 16b purposes.

Prior to 1991, the exercise was considered the purchase. In 1991, however, the Securities and Exchange Commission (SEC) decided correctly that the grant of ESOs rather than the exercise should be the purchase, subject to Securities Exchange Act Section 16b. This was done so by Rule 16 b(3).

Please visit: www.law.uc.edu/CCL/34ActRls/rule16b-3.html to view this section.

Prior to exemptions to Section 16b by SEC rule makers, it was a bit awkward to manage a portfolio of ESOs. But it could be done reasonably well, especially if the executive was interested in holding the ESOs for an extended period, as the plan was designed to achieve.

But, like everyone else, executives want to buy low and sell high. This meant trying to be granted options with low strike prices and sell stock at a high price. But 16b was interfering with their executive's desires to backdate and spring-load and then manipulate the price higher so they could sell high. In 1991, exemptions were made for grants of ESOs, conditioned upon approval by boards, compensation committees, or shareholders and certain restrictions imposed on the grantee. These 1991 exemptions granted some relief to executives, but not enough for them to be happy. Please visit: http://content.lawyerlinks.com/default.htm# http://content.lawyerlinks.com/library/sec/sec_releases/34-34513.htm to view this. Also see: www.law.uc.edu/CCL/34ActRls/rule16b-3.html.

Even with the 1991 exemptions, the executives still had trouble backdating and spring-loading with 16b in the way. In 1996, the SEC modified the qualifications to broaden exemptions in order to accommodate the desires of executives and their advisers.

This opened the doors for backdating, spring-loading, and earnings manipulations to accommodate executive grants, and artificially disguised reloading of the exercised ESOs.

Further SEC Encouragement, 1996

In 1996, the SEC even considered asking Congress to rescind Section 16b altogether and requested comments on that point. Essentially, the SEC asked for comments from the foxes guarding the henhouse to determine how the foxes could best guard the hens. Of course, the foxes did not want it to appear that they got every concession. Otherwise, the hens would discover the game.

After 1996, if Rule 16b(3)(d) exemptions are interpreted in the manner as some experts promote, every grant of ESOs that was issued since 1996 is exempt from Section 16b whether or not it was approved by shareholders, the board of directors, or compensation committees. According to attorneys for the foxes, if an options grant has a vesting period of six months or longer it is automatically exempt from Section 16b, even if there was no approval from anyone. In some rare instances, options are granted with no vesting period. What could be the reasoning behind such a lack of a vesting period if not to exercise shortly after a backdating, or a spring-load, or an intention to exercise very soon after the grant?

Please visit: http://content.lawyerlinks.com/ default.htm#http://content.lawyerlinks.com/library/sec/sec_releases/34-34513.htm for more information.

Extreme Abuses Accommodated by the SEC

Assume that on April 1, 2006, an executive is granted 3 million options (with a 12-month vesting period) to "purchase the underlying stock," which the executive does not and cannot exercise until after April 1, 2007. The grant day is one day before very positive news is announced at the close on April 2, 2006.

Assume also that he held 2 million options on February 28, 2006, from grants made years earlier. Assume that on April 7, 2006, he exercises the 2 million options that he was granted years earlier and sells the 2 million shares of common stock on April 9, 2006, which he received from the exercise of earlier granted options. Assume the sale price of the 2 million shares on April 9, 2006 is 50 percent higher than the exercise price of the 3 million options grant made on April 1, 2006.

Some experts claim that even if there is no approval of the grant by the shareholders, the board of directors, or the compensation committee, the grant of April 1, 2006, is exempt from Section 16b and no recovery is allowed. According to some experts, the grant of April 1, 2006 is exempt because the executive did not exercise those options and sell the exact stock received from the exercise of the April 1, 2006 grant within six months of the grant.

This interpretation essentially vitiates Section 16b of the Securities Exchange Act of 1934, and allows and encourages insider trading. The whole purpose of backdating and spring-loading is to create an artificially low grant price and to sell stock shortly afterward at higher prices. Section 16b of the Securities Exchange Act of 1934 made that practice far less attractive. So the SEC accommodated the executives and promulgated Rule 16b(3) of 1996. Whether the SEC was aware of the consequences of the 1996 Rule 16b(3) or they were duped, the result is the same.

Conclusion

Without the 1996 Rule 16b(3), the backdating and spring-loading by executives would be very small, and certainly not what we have seen. Did

Rule 16b(3) cause or contribute to the proliferation of backdating grants and exercises, spring-loading, bullet dodging, manipulating earnings to accommodate grants and stock sales, and disguised reloading? The view of the authorities is that it did. And that is why most of the backdating and other options scams are dated between 1996 and 2002. We doubt, however, whether the SEC will agree. They blame it on lack of proper gatekeeping by the compensation committees of the board of directors.

Glossary

Alternative Minimum Tax (AMT) A term that refers to a tax assessable against a holder of qualified ESOs upon exercise. AMT is widely discussed in books on managing ESOs. Hedging ESOs to reduce risk with listed calls and puts minimizes the concern for the AMT, because we advise not making exercises of ESOs until near expiration. The resulting gain from a focus on the AMT is minimal compared to the gain from merely delaying the exercise to expiration.

American-Style Option Most listed calls are American-style options and can be exercised anytime after purchase. If a person is short American calls, he or she may be assigned the options contract at any time. But most listed calls are assigned on the last day before expiration, or they expire out-of-the-money and worthless. All employee stock options become American-style options once they vest.

Assignment This happens when a person has written and is short listed calls or puts. Expiration date gets near or there is some extraordinary reason, and holders of the listed puts and calls exercise their listed options. The exercise notices go to the Options Clearing Corporation (OCC), and the OCC randomly assigns that exercise notice to a writer of calls or a writer of puts.

At-the-Money An option is at-the-money if the exercise price equals or is very near the market price of the stock.

Backdating An illegal practice carried out by executives who seek to extract excessive gains from the company they work for. It involves issuing employee stock options with exercise prices lower than they should be by choosing an earlier day as the grant day when the stock was lower than on the grant day.

Bearish Position A position in stock or options whereby the summed total deltas are negative and the deltas are expected to stay negative as the stock price changes.

Black-Scholes Model The first theoretical options pricing model, for which two of its creators won the Nobel Prize in 1997. The model suggests prices for listed stock options based on expectations of stock prices moving according to geometric Brownian motion. It is widely used by listed options traders and appraisers of ESOs. There are some experts that dispute the accuracy of this model, especially when dealing with long-term options on high-volatility stocks. Myron Scholes and Bill Merton, the Nobel Prize recipients, were principals in the ill-fated Long Term Capital Management hedge fund.

Blackout Period A period in which executives are restricted from buying or selling equity securities of their employer. Blackout periods are instituted by the company to comply with Securities and Exchange Commission mandates against insider trading by company executives.

Bullish Position   A position in stock or options whereby the summed total deltas are positive and are expected to remain positive as the stock price changes.

Butterfly Spread   A strategy involving three strike prices that has limited risk and limited potential gain.

Calendar Spread or Time Spread   A combination of two positions in listed options that have the same strike price but with different times to expiration.

Call   An option that gives the holder the right to buy stock at a specific price throughout a specific period. One listed call usually gives the right to purchase 100 shares of stock. All employee and executive stock options are similar to calls. Listed call options are contracts with the Options Clearing Corporation. Employee and executive stock options are contracts with the employer.

Cash Settlement   Some options and some stock appreciation rights settle in cash, not in securities. Upon exercise, the optionee receives the intrinsic value of the options in cash.

CBOE   The Chicago Board Options Exchange, the largest options trading floor in the world.

Closing Transaction   A trade that closes an existing open position. If a person writes calls and later buys the same calls, he has executed a closing transaction.

Collar   A collar consists of the simultaneous selling of an out-of-the-money listed call and buying of an out-of-the-money listed put with the same expiration dates. This combination of options trades is usually done when the trader wants to protect the long position in his stock or employee options. Given the fact that there are large numbers of owners of stock positions who decide to execute collar strategies, there is pressure on the market price of the out-of-the-money calls (especially the longer-term out-of-the-money calls) to sell below the theoretical values. The out-of-the-money puts generally trade above their theoretical value. So executing collars requires quite a concession to the theoretical values and add extra transaction costs to hedging.

Constructive Sale   The sale or short sale or writing of an option or future that the IRS considers to be essentially a sale of the underlying security itself, causing an immediate taxable event.

Conversion   The simultaneous purchase of stock plus the sale of a call and purchase of a put with the same exercise price and expiration date.

Cover   To buy back a short position in an option. Sometimes traders are forced to "cover" a position when they are overextended.

Covered Calls   Listed calls that have been written against long stock or against offsetting different calls. Sometimes the sale of puts versus the sale of calls can be considered covered positions. Employee stock options start as naked calls and become covered when a sale is made of listed calls with expiration periods shorter than the ESOs.

Delta   The amount that a call option should increase for every point that the stock increases, and the amount the call option should decrease for every point that the stock decreases over a short period of time.

Delta Risk   The effective stock equivalency of the portfolio of options and stock positions. The delta risk can be long or short or neutral.

Employee Stock Options   Contracts between the employee and the employer that give the employee the right, but not the obligation, to purchase common stock from the employer for a specific price throughout a specific period of time. The maximum expiration date is fixed on the grant day but may change if the employee decides to terminate or is terminated earlier than expiration day. The maximum expiration day is generally ten years from the grant date.

Equivalent Stock Position   Every option has a delta (i.e., an amount that the option is expected to move for every one point move of the stock). The equivalent stock position means the summed total of all the stock and options positions. If a person owns 5,000 shares of Microsoft and has just written 50 calls each with a .50 delta, the equivalent stock position is now +2,500.

Erosion   What happens to employee and listed options as time passes and the time premium wears away. Erosion of ESOs can be mitigated by selling listed options with exercise prices similar to the ESOs.

ESOs   Employee (or executive) stock options issued by the company to employees and executives as compensation.

Exercise Price   The price at which you have the right to purchase the common stock from the company in the case of ESOs, or from the Options Clearing Corporation in the case of listed options. Sometimes this price is referred to as the strike price. Sometimes in the case of ESOs the company may offer to adjust the strike price along with respective adjustments in the number of options granted.

Expected Time to Expiration   The "expected" expiration date of employee options. There is always a possibility that the ESOs will be prematurely exercised or the employee may terminate prior to vesting. Appraisers of ESOs reduce the maximum time to expiration and get what is called the expected time to expiration.

Expense Options   What the company does when it calculates the full value of ESOs and writes off that value of the granted ESOs against earnings. Companies are required to follow the rules of the Financial Accounting Standards Board when reporting income on their financial statements.

Expiration Date   The date on which the options expire. After this date, the options, if not exercised, will be worthless. Employees must clearly exercise their options in the case of ESOs, even if the options are substantially in-the-money. Sometimes the expiration date for ESOs changes if the employee is prematurely terminated. In the case of listed options, the brokerage firm will automatically exercise the options if they are in-the-money by at least one cent.

Fair Market Value   The price at which an identical or very similar asset or security would be selling in the marketplace at any given time between fully informed buyers and sellers.

FASB   Financial Accounting Standards Board; the designated organization in the private sector for establishing standards of financial accounting and reporting. The FASB is officially recognized as authoritative by the Securities and Exchange Commission and the American Institute of Certified Public Accountants. The FASB sets the standards as to how ESOs are to be accounted for.

Forfeiture of Time Premium   One of the consequences of premature exercises of ESOs. The forfeited time premium goes to the employer.

Grant Date   The day on which the employer grants to the employee the rights that he has under the terms of the option contract. The maximum contractual expiration day is usually ten years from the grant date. An options contract between the employee and the employer is created on the grant date, requiring future performance by both parties.

Hedge   A conservative strategy used to limit investment loss by effecting a transaction that offsets an existing position.

Hedging Naked Employee Options   What informed employees do when they want to reduce the risk of owning ESOs. This is done by either writing listed calls, shorting stock, buying listed puts, or doing collars. Writing listed calls is the most effective means of reducing the risk of holding ESOs, although under many circumstances buying puts alone or in combination with sales of calls can best achieve the desired results. These "hedging transactions" are done through a broker and can most efficiently be accomplished through an online broker. There are few ESO consultants who understand the process, and few advise the strategy. Hedging employee options is the only way to maximize the options, value, reduce risk, and minimize taxes.

Implied Volatility   A phrase that is used by many options practitioners who claim that the present market price of the options implies information about the future volatility of the stock. When the options are trading in the marketplace different from the Black-Scholes theoretical values, observers say the implied volatility is higher or lower than the model suggests. This is based on the idea that the models are accurate. In fact, the models are, to a degree, inaccurate. When the options in the market are different from the theoretical values, this implies not only something having to do with different volatilities. It also implies that the models are inaccurate and the market is trying to correct those errors by adjusting the market prices accordingly.

In-the-Money   An expression used to describe a listed call or employee stock option that has an exercise price less than the market price of the stock. All employee options are call options. In the case of a put, the in-the-money put has an exercise price greater than the market price. The amount of in-the-moneyness is called the intrinsic value of the option.

Incentive Options   Options that must satisfy a list of requirements of the tax law. The options must have an exercise price equal to or above the market price of the stock when issued, and the exercise date cannot be longer than ten years.

Insider Trading   There are two kinds of insider trading: (1) the illegal kind, where a person buys or sells stock with material, nonpublic information; and (2) the kind done by directors and officers when not deemed illegal.

Intrinsic Value   That part of the option equal to the difference between the exercise price of the option and the market price of the stock. The intrinsic value can never be below zero. This is the amount that the option is "in-the-money." At expiration date, the intrinsic value equals the full theoretical value of the options.

IRAs and Roth IRAs An IRA is an individual retirement account, and a Roth is a particular type of individual retirement account. IRAs can be used in the management of a person's ESOs with the best tax consequences. An employee with an IRA can buy puts in an IRA to hedge the risk in holding his or her naked ESOs. For a number of reasons, using IRAs to manage ESOs is the absolute best way to achieve the lowest tax.

LEAPS (Long-Term Equity Anticipation Securities) Listed long-term stock or index options with expiration dates up to three years in the future. These are the calls most appropriate for writing against ESOs, especially the out-of-the-money calls in high-volatility stocks.

Limit Orders The kinds of orders that should be entered when trading options. Never enter market orders to buy or sell options. In fact, even when you trade stock, you should generally enter only limit orders.

Listed Options Options that are traded on the various options exchanges around the country and the world such as the Chicago Board Options Exchange and the International Stock Exchange. Listed options means the same as exchange traded calls and puts.

Lognormal Price Distributions The statistical distribution that some assume is representative of how stock prices move. It assumes that the price of a stock can go up indefinitely. It also assumes that if a stock went from $10 to $100 in three years, it has just as good as chance of going to $1,000 as it does to go back to $10 in the next three years.

Margin Account A person must open a margin account at a brokerage firm in order to effectively hedge his portfolio of ESOs. This account will allow him to short stock and write listed calls and buy listed puts. Most large brokerage firms discourage hedging ESOs by writing calls.

Margin Requirement The amount of cash or equivalents that is necessary to be advanced to purchase stock or options. When purchasing securities on margin, traders borrow the difference. When they short sell stock or write options, the margin plus the proceeds from the writing of calls is credited to the trader's account, upon which he earns interest.

Market Maker A person who stands on the trading floor at options exchanges or trades electronically and maintains bid and ask prices for the various options. He tries to earn a profit by selling the options for more than he paid or will pay. Some market makers try to make profits by being "theoretical traders." There are few opportunities for theoretical trading today.

Market Options Order The kind of orders that traders and employees should never place. Always use limit orders when trading listed options. Brokerage firms want clients to trade "at the market" because that helps their proprietary traders make money.

Naked Options Options that are uncovered or unhedged. One can be short naked listed options or long naked listed options. An owner of ESOs that are unhedged is an employee who owns naked employee options.

Naked Short Sale A short sale made when the seller does not borrow the shares sold and does not deliver shares. This type of sale is generally illegal but it is not enforced by the Securities and Exchange Commission.

Options Agreement   An agreement in which the specific terms of the options contract are spelled out regarding the number of shares that a grantee has a right to buy, the specific exercise price, the maximum time to expiration, and the vesting period. All grantees should examine this agreement in detail.

Options Clearing Corporation   The entity with whom owners and writers of listed stock options have a contract. The Options Clearing Corporation is obligated to deliver shares upon exercise of listed calls and is obligated to purchase shares upon exercise of listed puts (see Appendix A).

Ordinary Gain or Loss   The tax treatment of profits from nonqualified ESOs if IRS Section 1221 applies. Most tax lawyers and accountants believe that hedging by the use of listed options generally causes a capital gain or loss in the options used in hedging. Profits from long positions in puts and calls held for more than one year are generally treated as long-term capital gains.

Out-of-the-Money Options   These are options where the stock is trading below the exercise price of employee stock options or the exercise price of listed calls. Some refer to this as options being underwater. These options have no intrinsic value but do have time premium, the amount of which depends on a number of factors, including the volatility, the time remaining to expiration, and the price of the stock. Employees can effectively sell their out-of-the-money options by writing (i.e., selling) similar listed calls.

Overpriced Options   Listed options that are selling in the market for an amount greater than they should. At one time an overpriced option was thought to be one selling higher than the Black-Scholes model suggests. Now, since it is understood that the Black-Scholes model has errors, finding overpriced options to sell is more complicated. When we find overpriced options, we sell them and hedge the risk.

Premature Exercise   The exercising of options prior to the time they should be exercised. Premature exercise of employee options is the biggest mistake an employee can make. Usually, the options should be exercised at the last minute (except for far-in-the-money puts or in-the-money calls when a special dividend is expected or a tender offer has been made). This is the case with listed options and ESOs. Most investment advisers, accountants, and benefits planners erroneously advise the premature exercise of these ESOs. Premature exercises by employees and executives forfeit billions of dollars every year and cause a premature tax bill of even more. Employees who avoid premature exercises have 50 percent of the work accomplished in the proper management of their options.

Put   An options contract that allows the holder to sell the stock at a specific price during a period until expiration day. Generally, a put is issued by the Options Clearing Corporation on 100 shares. There are no employee put options.

Qualified Covered Call   A "qualified covered call" must meet three basic requirements: (1) the call cannot be too much in-the-money; (2) the calls must be listed on an options exchange, and (3) the calls must have at least 30 days remaining to expiration but not more than 33 months when sold (written). If the option had more than 12 months to expiration, the strike price would have to be adjusted to comply with the "covered call status" to comply with recent Treasury Regulations.

Readily Ascertainable   Options have a value when granted, but that value is ordinarily not readily ascertainable unless the option is actively traded on an established market. If an option is actively traded on an established market, the fair market value is readily ascertainable for purposes of IRS Section 83. For the purposes of Section 1.83-7, if an option is not traded on an established market, the option does not have a readily ascertainable fair market value when granted unless the taxpayer can show that all of the following conditions exist: (1) the option is transferable by the optionee; (2) the option is exercisable immediately in full by the optionee; (3) the option or the property subject to the option is not subject to any restriction or condition (other than a lien or other condition to secure the payment of the purchase price) that has a significant effect on the fair market value of the option; and (4) the fair market value of the option privilege is readily ascertainable in accordance with paragraph (b)(3) of this Section.

Restricted Stock   Restricted stock is the common stock of a company that is granted to an employee often as equity compensation but cannot be sold until the restricted stock vests. Many firms are using restricted stock to replace all or part of their future options grants. The most notable company to go down that road is Microsoft. Restricted stock in lieu of ESOs puts the recipient in a less risky position. But with less risk, the potential rewards are a lot less to the recipient.

Restricted Stock Units (RSUs)   A grant valued in terms of company stock, but company stock is not issued at the time of the grant. After the recipient of a unit satisfies the vesting requirement, the company distributes shares, or the cash equivalent of the number of shares used to value the unit. Depending on plan rules, the participant or grantee may be allowed to choose whether to settle in stock or cash.

Returns   Returns are technically defined as equal to the logarithm of the stock price relatives. Returns are not percentage gains. If a stock increases 10 percent, the return equals +9.53 percent. Most theoretical pricing models assume that returns are normally distributed.

Rollback   The simultaneous buying back of a previously sold near-term listed call option and selling a different listed option with a longer expiration date. A trader does this to reduce taxes and risk, and fine-tune the hedging of his ESOs.

Stock Appreciation Rights (SARs)   A right, usually granted to an employee, to receive a bonus equal to the appreciation in the company's stock over a specified period. Like ESOs, SARs benefit the holder depending upon an increase in stock price. The difference is that the employee is not required to pay the exercise price (as with an ESO), but rather just receives the amount of the increase in cash or stock.

Short Sale   An investor's making a bet that the stock will go down. This involves the borrowing of shares from an owner and selling those shares in the market. The proceeds of the sale are deposited in a special account where the brokerage firm earns interest. Sometimes, if he is a preferred client, the firm will give up to 80 percent of the interest earned in that account to the client. If the stock goes down, the short seller wins. If the stock goes up, the short seller loses. Shorting stock should be a consistently used tool by (noninsider) owners of ESOs. There are tax advantages to shorting stock. Company insiders are generally prohibited from shorting stock.

Straddle Rule   An IRS rule designed to stop creative tax avoiders. Assume a trader buys a call and simultaneously sells an offsetting call on a stock that is volatile. He is set up to have one position have a gain and the other have a loss when the stock moves. He could then close the loss and report an artificial loss but, in fact, he has no loss considering both positions. So the IRS says that when there are offsetting positions, any closed-out losses must be reduced by the unrecognized gain that accrues on the other position or the offsetting positions can be considered as "identified straddles" with different tax treatment.

Theoretical Value   The value of an option (whether listed or employee) that is produced if we assume that the pricing model is correct. The market price of listed options often differs from the theoretical value. Theoretical pricing models were designed for listed short-term options. However, with the proper corrections of the time to expiration and volatility assumptions, the models can be used to price ESOs.

Tight Market   A situation that occurs when the bid and offer for a listed option is very small, enabling traders to keep transaction costs to a minimum.

Time Premium   That part of the option value that is over and above the intrinsic value. The ESO's value at the day of grant consists of 100 percent of time premium. Time premium is that part of the value of an option that considers that to own the option requires less money than to own the shares. Time premium is also that part of the option's value that considers the fact that a person can lose a lot more money by owning shares than by owning an option to purchase the shares. The time premium is determined by the time remaining to expiration, the future expected volatility of the stock, the exercise price, the interest rate, the dividend, and the value of the stock. At expiration day there is no time premium. The time premium is what is forfeited to the employer when a person exercises his ESOs prematurely. Tens of billions of dollars of time premium are forfeited back to the company as a result of bad advice from options advisers.

Time Spread   When a trader, investor, or employee holds long a call or ESO and sells (writes) a listed call with the same strike price but with a shorter expiration day, he or she is considered to be an owner of a time spread.

Time to Expiration   The amount of time that remains in the life of the listed or employee options. In the case of listed options, the time to expiration is fixed. In the case of ESOs, the time to expiration can change. Employees tend to exercise their options prematurely due to a desire to reduce risk, or get the money. Also, if the employee is terminated voluntarily or nonvoluntarily, the expiration date will be accelerated to a much shorter time remaining.

Underlying Security   The same as "underlying equity security" as used in the Securities and Exchange Commission (SEC) rules and in Section 16 of the Securities Exchange Act of 1934. It means a security that relates to or is the subject of an option. This definition is from SEC Rule 12a(6).

Underpriced Options   Listed options that are selling in the market for less than they should. To make a determination of when an option is truly underpriced requires more than a comparison of the market price with the Black-Scholes theoretical values.

Vest A grantee's options vest when the grantee obtains the unrestricted right to own the options and generally the right to immediately exercise the granted ESOs. Often, the employee options vest 25 percent or 20 percent per year over a four- or five-year period. Listed options vest immediately.

VIX An index that was created by the Chicago Board Options Exchange for the ostensible purpose of gauging the implied volatility in the broad market. It fails to accomplish its objective for reasons beyond the scope of this definition. However, many traders and commentators follow it. Their relying on the VIX sometimes presents opportunities for the informed trader to exploit.

Volatility A measure of historical movements of the stock or stock indexes, with the idea that historical volatilities can be used to predict future volatilities. Technically, volatility equals the standard deviation of the returns of the stock. This technical measurement is used to predict the future expected volatility of the stock and the expected values of employee stock options.

Write Calls A person writes a listed call when he enters into an agreement with the Options Clearing Corporation (OCC) to sell a specific number of shares at a specific price. This can be done only with listed calls. For every owner of options, there is an equivalent writer. All listed options are contracts between the person and the OCC, whereas all employee options are contracts between the employee and the employer. Writing a call or a put is often referred to as selling a call or put.

Index